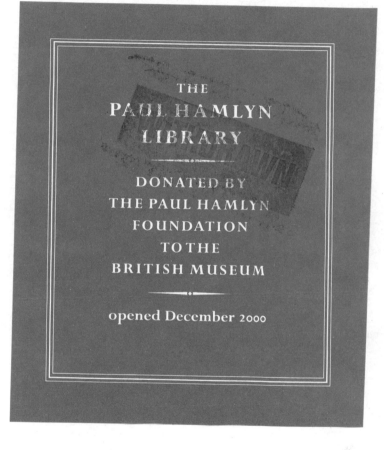

# THOMAS HARDY'S
## 'STUDIES, SPECIMENS &C.'
### NOTEBOOK

Lucr: the gliding constellations : unveil
the day, open the day, uncover the day :
spring into sight, life : fling upon, fling at :
crisis of eyes & heat : this system of pain :
1 Sam. 26 - to tell on, upon ; said
in my heart :

Swin : the thing beforetime seen : from
the midmost of Ida : I shall never be
friends again with roses. ( beauty here from
contrast of colloq. phrase with high thought. )

    fair     deep
    face    thought

overblown : bared thy beauties to : fain ( high )
a pres. introd by 'where' — .
    As the lost white feverish limbs *
    of the lesbian Sappho, adrift
    In foam where the seaweed swims #
    Swam loose for the streams to lift

You kill men's hearts : carve ( make ) :
whet : dumb under axe or dart : on this
wise : gone thorough ( through ) a privy way :

# Thomas Hardy's
# 'Studies, Specimens &c.'
# Notebook

Edited by

PAMELA DALZIEL

and

MICHAEL MILLGATE

CLARENDON PRESS · OXFORD

1994

Oxford University Press, Walton Street, Oxford OX2 6DP
Oxford New York Toronto
Delhi Bombay Calcutta Madras Karachi
Kuala Lumpur Singapore Hong Kong Tokyo
Nairobi Dar es Salaam Cape Town
Melbourne Auckland Madrid
and associated companies in
Berlin Ibadan

Oxford is a trade mark of Oxford University Press

Published in the United States
by Oxford University Press Inc., New York

British Library Cataloguing in Publication Data
Data available

Library of Congress Cataloging in Publication Data
Hardy, Thomas, 1840–1928.
[Studies, specimens &c. notebook]
Thomas Hardy's Studies, specimens &c. notebook / edited by Pamela
Dalziel and Michael Millgate.
Includes bibliographical references (p.) and index.
1. Hardy, Thomas, 1840–1928—Notebooks, sketchbooks, etc.
I. Dalziel, Pamela. II. Millgate, Michael. III. Title.
IV. Title: Studies, specimens &c notebook.
V. Title: Studies, specimens, etc. notebook.
PR4750.S78 1994 828'.803—dc20 93–8653
ISBN 0–19–811757–4

Set by Hope Services (Abingdon) Ltd.
Printed in Great Britain
on acidfree paper by
Biddles Ltd
Guildford & King's Lynn

# Acknowledgements

THE 'Studies, Specimens &c.' notebook was for many years in the collection of the late Richard Little Purdy, and its present editors would wish their edition to stand as a tribute to his memory and to his achievement as a scholar, editor, and collector.

The notebook was willed by Richard Purdy to the Beinecke Rare Book and Manuscript Library of Yale University, and the final stages of textual and bibliographical work upon it have been greatly facilitated by the co-operation of the Beinecke staff and especially of Vincent Giroud, the Curator of Modern Manuscripts. Marjorie Wynne, formerly of the Beinecke Library, has also been generously helpful in many ways, both direct and indirect, and the editors regret their inability to thank by name the unknown compiler of a type-script containing preliminary identifications of many of the notebook's quotations that was found amongst Richard Purdy's papers.

The editors can and do thank the following institutions and their staffs for permitting access to relevant materials and for advice and assistance, always cheerfully given: the British Library, especially Sally Brown and Elizabeth James; Colby College Library, especially Patience-Anne W. Lenck; the Dorset County Museum, especially Roger Peers; and the libraries of the University of British Columbia and the University of Toronto. They also jointly and severally acknowledge the assistance of Jane Cooper, Elaine Engst, George Fayen, J. D. Fleeman, Patricia Fleming, Robert H. Hirst, J. R. de J. Jackson, John M. Robson, Dennis Taylor, and Margaret Webster, and are particularly grateful to Frederick and Marie-Louise Adams for access to their collections and for hospitality and friendship, shown in so many ways; to Ann Payne (of the British Library) for her help in unravelling the mysteries of Hardy's shorthand; to Lesley Mann, for her indefatigable pursuit of some of Hardy's more recondite quotations; to Adrian Bond, for his efficient and imaginative research assistance; to Bill and Vera Jesty for their help, hospitality, and kindness over many years; and to Jane Millgate for her active support and scholarly advice.

It is, finally, a pleasure to record the editors' appreciation of the generous funding of work on this project by the Social Sciences and Humanities Research Council of Canada and the Isaac Walton

Killam Foundation. Their thanks are also due to the Trustees of the Will of Eva Anne Dugdale, proprietors of the Hardy copyrights, for permission to publish the 'Studies, Specimens &c.' notebook in its entirety.

Pamela Dalziel
Michael Millgate

# Contents

# List of Abbreviations

| | |
|---|---|
| Adams | Collection of Frederick B. Adams |
| Beinecke | Beinecke Rare Book and Manuscript Library, Yale University |
| *Biography* | Michael Millgate, *Thomas Hardy: A Biography* (Oxford: Oxford University Press, 1982) |
| Colby | Colby College, Waterville, Maine |
| DCM | Dorset County Museum, Dorchester, Dorset |
| *Letters* | *The Collected Letters of Thomas Hardy*, ed. Richard L. Purdy and Michael Millgate, 7 vols. (Oxford: Clarendon Press, 1978–88) |
| *Life* | Thomas Hardy, *The Life and Work of Thomas Hardy*, ed. Michael Millgate (London: Macmillan, 1984) |
| *LitN* | *The Literary Notebooks of Thomas Hardy*, ed. Lennart A. Björk, 2 vols. (London: Macmillan, 1985) |
| *OED* | *The Oxford English Dictionary* |
| *PersN* | *The Personal Notebooks of Thomas Hardy*, ed. Richard H. Taylor (London: Macmillan, 1978) |
| TH | Thomas Hardy |
| Wessex Edn. | *The Works of Thomas Hardy in Prose and Verse*, 24 vols. (London: Macmillan, 1912–31) |

# Introduction

THE archive of Thomas Hardy manuscript materials is in certain respects satisfyingly large: pre-publication forms are extant for almost all of his books, both prose and verse, and his *Collected Letters* run to seven volumes. But there are also deplorable absences: letters dating from Hardy's first four decades are in short supply, no more than a dozen seeming to have survived from the period prior to 1870, the year of his thirtieth birthday, and he himself ensured in old age the destruction of those working diary-notebooks—full of ideas and plots for projected stories, outlines, images, and prosodic models for possible poems, and observations of people, places, and things—that he had kept from the 1860s until at least the early years of the twentieth century. With the exception of some school workbooks, a few fragments excised from documents otherwise destroyed, and the 'Schools of Painting' and 'Architectural' notebooks—both devoted to factual and technical matters[1]—the only early notebook materials generally available to scholars have been the brief extracts Hardy preserved in the first of his 'Literary Notes' notebooks[2] or transferred (with or without revision) either into the 'Life' of himself that was eventually published, after his death, over the name of his second wife[3] or into one or other of the 'synthetic' collections of still unused and potentially usable materials that he compiled, late in his career, while systematically revisiting the diary-notebooks prior to their destruction.[4]

Given this paucity of notebook material and of early documentation in general, the importance of the 'Studies, Specimens &c.' notebook can scarcely be exaggerated. Although not one of the diary-notebooks, it stands almost alone as a witness to Hardy's exertions and aspirations in the mid-1860s, when he was still working in London as an assistant to a prominent architect and tentatively feeling his way towards as yet dimly glimpsed possibilities of literary

---

[1] See *PersN*, xviii–xx, and *The Architectural Notebook of Thomas Hardy*, ed. C. J. P. Beatty (Dorchester: Dorset Natural History and Archaeological Society, 1966).
[2] *LitN*, I.3–7.  [3] See *Life*, xiv–xvi.
[4] See the earlier of the two 'Memoranda' notebooks included in *PersN* and the references in *Biography*, 89–90, to a 'Poetical Matter' notebook; although the original of the latter appears to have been lost or destroyed a microfilm is now available in Beinecke.

expression and employment. And while the notebook contains no drafts of actual poems, it is of extraordinary interest as providing detailed evidence of the ways in which Hardy, already in his middle twenties, was seeking to provide himself with a poetic background, educate himself in poetic techniques, and initiate a process from which he might just possibly emerge as a practising, perhaps even a publishing, poet.

That so intimate a document should have survived at all is itself remarkable given Hardy's instinct for privacy, the combustion within his own lifetime of so many records of his personal and creative past (including a considerable number of the diary-notebooks), and his apparent insistence—not in his will but in separate instructions that seem not to have survived—upon the posthumous destruction of all remaining notebooks, excepting only the temporary survival of material needed by his widow for the completion of the 'Life'. Sydney Cockerell, who shared with Florence Hardy the responsibilities of the literary executorship, seems to have been opposed as a matter of principle to the preservation of notes, drafts, and other witnesses of literary work-in-progress, and he did indeed burn in the fireplace of Hardy's study many documents still in existence at the time of Hardy's death.[5] Even Cockerell, however, appears to have recognized the appropriateness of retaining certain materials until the 'Life' should have been written, and it was presumably that provision of Hardy's which permitted the survival not only of the 'Memoranda' notebooks, specifically designed to provide both distant and recent material for Florence Hardy's biographical use and since edited by Richard H. Taylor as the *Personal Notebooks*, but also of such systematic accumulations—commonplace books rather than notebooks for everyday use—as the so-called 'Literary' notebooks, those important records of his reading since edited by Lennart A. Björk, and the as yet unedited 'Facts' notebook, a highly miscellaneous collection of contemporary news items and details of local history drawn for the most part from newspapers and magazines.[6]

Since the 'Studies, Specimens &c.' notebook fell only marginally into this latter category, its long-term preservation was fortunate

[5] See Millgate, *Testamentary Acts: Browning, Tennyson, James, Hardy* (Oxford: Clarendon Press, 1992), 157–61.

[6] See the description in *LitN*, I.xxxi; the notebook itself, in DCM, was reproduced by EP Microform on Reel 9 of their microfilm collection, 'The Original Manuscripts and Papers of Thomas Hardy', issued in 1975.

indeed. Though marked for destruction, it must have remained for Hardy an especially poignant memento of his early literary struggles: Florence Hardy certainly appreciated its importance, and took steps to ensure its passage, upon her death, into the hands of Richard Little Purdy, the young bibliographer from Yale whom she had learned to value both for his scholarly devotion to her husband's memory and for the personal friendship that had developed between them during the course of his several visits to Max Gate from 1929 onwards. 'Studies, Specimens &c.' remained a centrepiece of Purdy's extraordinary Hardy collection until his death in 1990, shown briefly to a few visiting scholars,[7] but always kept in reserve as an editorial project to be pursued following completion of the Clarendon Press edition of *The Collected Letters of Thomas Hardy*. By the terms of Purdy's will the notebook went with the rest of his collection to the Beinecke Library of Yale University, falling into place there alongside such other major items as the manuscript of *Human Shows*, presented to the library by Florence Hardy's sister in 1939, essentially at Purdy's instigation, and the manuscript of *Far from the Madding Crowd*, presented in 1989 by Edwin A. Thorne partly in recognition of Purdy's contribution to Hardy studies.

The front free-endpaper of 'Studies, Specimens &c.' bears Hardy's name, the address (16 Westbourne Park Villas) at which he lived for most of his initial London period of 1862–7,[8] and the date 1865. That date was perhaps a later addition of Hardy's—as may also have been the heading, '1865 Notes', inscribed and doubly underlined on the first page of entries—but there seems no reason to doubt that the earliest inscriptions in the notebook, perhaps even the bulk of the inscriptions overall, do indeed belong to that year. In a biographical outline Hardy supplied to the New York *Book Buyer* in 1892 he specifically identified 1865–7 as a period during which he 'read and wrote exclusively',[9] and in the largely autobiographical 'Life' he spoke especially of 1866 and 1867 as years during which he not only devoted himself to the reading of verse, as containing 'the essence of

---

[7] See, for example, *LitN*, I.xxxi, 267, 287, 365, etc., and *Biography*, 87–9.

[8] A note in one of Hardy's Bibles (DCM: see Romans 6) indicates that he moved into his room at 16 Westbourne Park Villas on 26 June 1863; he remained there until he left London itself in the summer of 1867.

[9] *Book Buyer* (New York), 9 (May 1892), 152; for Hardy's authorship see *Letters*, I.260.

all imaginative and emotional literature', but was 'constantly' writing it, though with no attempt at publication: 'by retaining his poems, and destroying those he thought irremediably bad—though he afterwards fancied he had destroyed too many—he may have been saved from the annoyance of seeing his early crude effusions crop up in later life'.[10]

The excision of several leaves at the end of the notebook renders it impossible to establish with any precision the date at which Hardy stopped using it. That the great majority of the entries antedate Hardy's departure from London in the summer of 1867 there can be no doubt, but since he pencilled his name, his Bockhampton address, and the date "67' on the verso of the notebook's front free-endpaper, and copied on to its final intact pages several brief extracts from the *Fortnightly Review* of January 1869, he evidently continued to make some use of it even after his return to Dorset. It is tempting, in view of that 1867 date, to postulate a possible link between 'Studies, Specimens &c.' and the extant literary commonplace book (included in Björk's edition of *Literary Notebooks*) which is similarly dated '1867' on its front endpaper. But the latter differs in size, has had many of its early leaves removed, and contains on its remaining leaves no material that can be confidently assigned to so early a date.[11] The one faint connection between the two notebooks depends upon the pencilled inscription, on one of the final pages of '1867', of the phrase 'Utilitarian romance'[12] and its suggestive similarity to the subtitle of Charles Reade's *Hard Cash: A Matter-of-Fact Romance*, a novel on which Hardy made a brief note in 'Studies, Specimens &c.' (70.11).[13]

It was apparently not long after Hardy's return from London to Bockhampton in 1867 that he began writing his never-to-be-published first novel *The Poor Man and the Lady*, and 'Studies, Specimens &c.' contains several hints, often frustratingly cryptic or incompletely legible, of Hardy's turning away from poetry in the years 1867–8 and re-directing his efforts toward the production of prose fiction, already initiated by the publication of 'How I Built

---

[10] *Life*, 51.

[11] *LitN*, I.xxxiv, speaks of the first 20 entries as 'possibly from the 1860s'.

[12] Millgate, *Thomas Hardy: His Career as a Novelist* (London: Bodley Head, 1971), 116, tentatively associates 'Utilitarian romance' with *The Hand of Ethelberta*.

[13] References to the page and line numbers of the present edition are given in this form throughout: see 'Editorial Procedures', xxvi.

Myself a House' in March 1865.[14] The rough sketch of a sanctimo-
niously puritanical figure at 78.1–14 seems clearly to have been written with a novel or short story in view, and vestiges of this initial
conception, though no precise verbal echoes, can perhaps be
detected in the figure of Elias Spinks in *Under the Greenwood Tree* and
even in that of Tony Kytes in 'A Few Crusted Characters', known
for his superficial seriousness and his capacity to sing an indecent
ballad 'with a religious manner, as if it were a hymn'.[15] Two pages
later in the notebook, at 80.1–3, there is a briefer, perhaps related,
suggestion for a comically self-important character based partly on
Costard in *Love's Labour's Lost* and partly on one Edward Cox, an
inhabitant of Higher Bockhampton during Hardy's childhood.[16] A
little later still (85.4) the note, 'Might begin a tale thus', is annexed in
shorthand to the heavily traditional opening of 'The Saga of
Gunnlaug the Worm-Tongue and Rafn the Skald' as it appeared in
the January 1869 *Fortnightly Review* over the names of Eiríkr
Magnússon and William Morris.

The quotations (86.8–87.15) from the liberal historian and cam-
paigner Goldwin Smith, extensive in themselves and identified by
page numbers as if in anticipation of a possible reconsultation, may
reflect a purely technical interest—Horace Moule having praised
Smith's style as '*very* good: & his vigour in argument firstrate'[17]—or
offer possible insights into Hardy's political views at the time of writing *The Poor Man and the Lady*, described in the 'Life' as having displayed tendencies that were 'socialistic, not to say revolutionary'.[18]
From some erased but still partly legible pencillings on the rear endpaper it further appears that Hardy currently had access, as a sub-
scriber, to the fiction-loaded shelves of Mudie's Select Library
and was proposing, in particular, to borrow a copy of *The Heir of
Redclyffe*, Charlotte M. Yonge's immensely popular novel of 1853—the

[14] See Thomas Hardy, *The Excluded and Collaborative Stories*, ed. Pamela Dalziel
(Oxford: Clarendon Press, 1992), 10–15.

[15] Hardy, *Life's Little Ironies* (Wessex Edn.), 194; also relevant is the brief description
of a relative of Bathsheba's that survives undeleted in the manuscript of *Far from the
Madding Crowd*, fo. 86 (Beinecke).

[16] That the two notes are connected is indicated by Hardy's having had Cox's
father in mind as the 'original' of Tony Kytes's father: see Simon Gatrell, *Hardy the
Creator: A Textual Biography* (Oxford: Clarendon Press, 1988), 116.

[17] Letter to Hardy, 21 Feb. 1864 (DCM), partly printed in Lois Deacon and Terry
Coleman, *Providence and Mr Hardy* (London: Hutchinson, 1966), 91.

[18] *Life*, 63.

probable source, incidentally, of the name 'Amabel' used in one of his earliest poems.[19]

Although the erased items on the rear endpaper—like those on page 84—could in theory belong to almost any period of Hardy's life, there is enough recoverable evidence to indicate that they were inscribed either during the 1865–8 period or shortly thereafter. Peculiar interest therefore attaches to some incompletely legible references to the placing of advertisements by Macmillan & Co. and to Hardy's discussions with George Lillie Craik, a partner in the Macmillan publishing house. These could conceivably relate to negotiations for the publication of *Under the Greenwood Tree* in 1871, but if, as seems likely, they are of earlier date, then the possibility exists that Macmillan & Co. were at one point more nearly committed to publishing *The Poor Man and the Lady*—or were believed by Hardy himself to be so committed—than has previously been assumed. An especially tantalizing note, 'Book | use "the lady Elfrid"', seems to suggest either that the name Elfride, later given to the heroine of *A Pair of Blue Eyes*, was at least temporarily assigned to the 'Lady' of *The Poor Man and the Lady* or that there may indeed be a solid basis for Hardy's insistence[20] that at least an outline of *A Pair of Blue Eyes*, with a Dorset setting and a different title, was already in existence at the moment in September 1872 when the story was first solicited and then accepted as a serial for *Tinsleys' Magazine*.[21]

That Hardy in the late 1860s nevertheless remained uncertain about his future becomes clear from a reference to Mark Lemon, editor of *Punch*, said in the 'Life' to have been consulted (apparently in late 1866 or early 1867) as to the prospects for theatrical employment as a route to the eventual writing of plays.[22] Hardy also reminds himself to ask Horace Moule about possible employment as a publisher's 'hack' (89.9 *inv.*), and records the resolution, should he not establish himself as a writer ('If lit. fails'), to fall back on a career in architecture, perhaps in an area such as Holderness (89.5–6 *inv.*), a part of south-eastern Yorkshire famous for its Gothic churches. Earlier in the notebook, in more confident mood, he had seemed to assure himself—in the face, perhaps, of parental opinion to the con-

---

[19] E. G. Withycombe, *The Oxford Dictionary of Christian Names*, 3rd edn. (Oxford: at the Clarendon Press, 1977), 18, identifies *The Heir of Redclyffe* as having contributed largely to the Victorian revival of 'Amabel' and other medieval names.
[20] *Life*, 77; see also *Biography*, 144 and n.     [21] *Letters*, I.17.     [22] *Life*, 55.

trary—that to abandon architecture if successful in literature would be 'not blameable but great' (59.1).

Suggestive though such biographical glimpses undoubtedly are, the interest and importance of 'Studies, Specimens &c.' lie above all in its direct revelation of the methods—earnest, laborious, and not always readily comprehensible—by which Hardy as a young man sought to educate himself in poetry and propel himself, as if by sheer effort, into the writing of verse. The later 'Literary Notes' notebooks emphasize by their very diligence and doggedness the continued presence of an autodidactic strain in Hardy, and there can be little doubt that he felt hampered in his career and in his social relationships by what he had come to think of as the inadequacy and incompleteness of his education. His Dorchester schooling, although far from contemptible for his time, place, and social class, had provided a better grounding for his original career as an architect than for the career in literature to which he now aspired, and it was awareness of his poor preparation in Latin and Greek as much as the obvious financial obstacles which led him in 1865 or 1866 to abandon, once and for all, his long-cherished hope of gaining admission to the University of Cambridge, taking orders, becoming 'a curate in a country village', and so 'combining poetry and the Church'.[23] The circumstances of Hardy's upbringing—despite his good fortune in encountering early on such remarkable figures as William Barnes and the various members of the Moule family—also constrained the scope and progress of his poetic ambitions. What the early portions of 'Studies, Specimens &c.' strongly suggest is that, for all his youthful reading and dedicated study, Hardy in 1865 still possessed only a meagre literary background and was signally lacking in the kind of linguistic and lexical competence that might be imagined as necessary to the writing of verse—or, indeed, to the pursuit of almost any literary career.[24] Many pages of the notebook are devoted to vocabulary-building exercises consisting of the quotation and selective underlining of brief snippets, rarely of more than three

---

[23] *Letters*, I.7; *Life*, 53, 52; and see *Life*, 38, for his having stopped studying Greek in the late 1850s.

[24] In striking contrast to 'Studies, Specimens &c.' are the exactly contemporary notebooks of Gerard Manley Hopkins, four years Hardy's junior: see *The Early Poetic Manuscripts and Note-Books of Gerard Manley Hopkins*, ed. Norman H. MacKenzie (New York: Garland Publishing, 1989).

or four words in length, taken for the most part from *The Golden Treasury* and from such solidly 'canonical' authors as Shakespeare, Spenser, Milton, Burns, Wordsworth, Scott, Coleridge, Byron, and Shelley—though also from such contemporaries as Tennyson, Jean Ingelow, and Swinburne.

The quotations themselves are highly miscellaneous and seem to have been chosen on no clear basis of principle or method. Perhaps not surprisingly, Hardy was often drawn to language of an obviously 'poetic' and even archaic sort—'unweeting' (4.14), 'while-ere' (4.17), 'neighbour nigh' (10.10–11), etc.—but he also quoted at some length from the Dorset dialect poems of William Barnes (42.16–43.2, 43.16–44.4, etc.) and when writing down words from memory (e.g. 'Recoll', for 'Recollections', at 22.2–9) he evidently saw no incongruity in including dialectal expressions—'quite the dand(y)' (22.5), for instance, which later resurfaced in *Far from the Madding Crowd*.[25] There are several instances of Hardy's copying out the same passage twice over (e.g. 23.8–9 and 28.13–14; 31.13–15 and 74.1–2; 57.13 and 74.9) and he was also capable, at least in the earlier pages of the notebook, not just of copying down but of emphasizing by underlining what seem on the face of it to be quite simple and familiar words and phrases—'rancour' (3.17), 'rapture' (3.18), 'aiding' (4.13), and 'timely' (5.13), for example, and 'pipe' (8.11) and 'deck' (8.13) as verbs. Words initially occurring within quotations often become absorbed into Hardy's own vocabulary (e.g. 'jocund' at 38.1 and 38.8), but even the later and more elaborate dictionary exercises (e.g. pp. 43, 45, 46) tend to confirm the impression of early lexical deprivation even while they simultaneously chart the earnest and persistent processes of enlargement and sophistication: such paragraphs as that at 45.1–12 headed 'Dic' (for 'Dictionary') and devoted to words beginning with the letter 'C' may have been suggested by Horace Moule's appointment to collect entries for the letter 'H' on behalf of the *New English Dictionary*.[26] Hardy soon began to insert brief memoranda into the notebook as he went along (e.g. 'one may be used = I' at 6.6), and it is at once fascinating and amusing to watch him identify the expansive possibilities of the suffix '-less' (23.15), a charac-

---

[25] Wessex Edn. 381; for still other occurrences see Ralph W. V. Elliott, *Thomas Hardy's English* (Oxford: Basil Blackwell, 1984), 91.

[26] K. M. Elisabeth Murray, *Caught in the Web of Words: James A. H. Murray and the Oxford English Dictionary* (New Haven, Conn.: Yale University Press, 1977), 175; though his assistance was acknowledged, Moule seems never to have produced any entries.

teristic feature of his verse in later years, or register, rather less pro-
ductively, that 'The plu[ral] often makes a common word novel as
grasses, dews' (54.17).

P. Austin Nuttall's *Standard Pronouncing Dictionary of the English
Language* was one of several important works that Hardy purchased in
1865 as part of that campaign of poetic self-education and self-
development to which 'Studies, Specimens &c.' is itself the most elo-
quent witness. Other surviving volumes dated 1865 in Hardy's hand
include John Walker's *Rhyming Dictionary*, Henry Reed's *Introduction to
English Literature*, and the poetical works of Milton, Thomson, and
Coleridge. He already owned the copy of Palgrave's *Golden Treasury*
that Horace Moule had given him in 1862, together with such
important items as a one-volume Wordsworth and a ten-volume
*Dramatic Works of William Shakespeare*; other titles, a Spenser, a Dryden,
and Shelley's *Queen Mab and Other Poems* among them, were added
during the Westbourne Park Villas period.[27] Part of the interest of
'Studies, Specimens &c.' lies, of course, in its supplementation of
existing knowledge of Hardy's early reading—the literary context
within which he located himself, by chance or design, at the time
when he first began to write—and whenever a surviving volume
from Hardy's library can be confidently identified as the immediate
source of quotations entered into the notebook it has been consulted
and cited in annotating the present edition. It is important to keep in
mind, however, that Hardy's markings in such copies and his quotations in the notebook would almost always have reflected separate
readings of the text and that he may sometimes have worked with
borrowed or library (i.e. non-circulating) copies even of titles that he
did already own.

Much of the material quoted in the notebook serves chiefly to
confirm, and make more specific, the importance of literary connec-
tions acknowledged by Hardy himself. The impact of Swinburne, for
example, is strongly signalled by the length of the passages from his
early poems which Hardy went to the trouble of writing out from a
friend's copy,[28] and the quotations from Shakespeare are not only

[27] With the exception of the Shelley (Adams), all the volumes mentioned in this
paragraph are now in DCM. For relevant observations on Hardy's use of these and
other early purchases see Dennis Taylor, 'Hardy's Missing Poem and his Copy of
Milton', *Thomas Hardy Journal*, 6 (Feb. 1990), 50–60.

[28] Florence Hardy, reporting this to Richard Purdy, added that Hardy later regret-
ted not having been obliged to buy *Poems and Ballads* in a potentially valuable first edition: Purdy, note of 11 Aug. 1935 (Beinecke).

numerous and various but often accompanied by memoranda that both endorse and illuminate Hardy's statement, many years later, that he read Shakespeare 'more closely from 23 to 26' than he had ever done since.[29] His enthusiasm for *Marmion* and Scott's poetry in general is also amply displayed, and it is intriguing to find one of the Waverley novels—*Kenilworth*, said to have been a favourite of Hardy's mother's[30]—as the only work of prose fiction ransacked for usable phrases (41.13–42.3). Some new names—Jean Ingelow, Isa Craig, and Robert Buchanan—do occur, however, the extent of Hardy's early interest in Barnes and Tennyson becomes a great deal clearer, and pages 8–11 of the notebook provide a remarkable demonstration of the degree to which he familiarized himself with at least the sixteenth- and seventeenth-century selections of *The Golden Treasury*—his urgent search for literary knowledge evidently leading him to seize upon that anthology as a supremely canonical source, its authority by no means diminished by the fact that his own copy had come from Horace Moule.[31] At the very end of his life Hardy would declare that his one literary ambition had been to have one or more of his poems included 'in a good anthology like the *Golden Treasury*'.[32]

Although the Shakespeare passages at the very beginning of the notebook are scrupulously laid out, its early pages otherwise display an almost complete disregard for the technical aspects of the poems being quoted, the vast majority of the entries neither constituting complete lines of verse nor incorporating any signals as to the presence of line-breaks. Quotations at the end of the notebook tend to be correctly set out, and in the middle sections some strongly rhythmic lines of Swinburne's are faithfully rendered (e.g. 55.5–57.18 and 64.5–66.2), but 'Studies, Specimens &c.' shows in general a lack of attention to such matters as metre, rhyme, and stanza form that may seem surprising in the light of Hardy's eventual exploitation in his own verse of an exceptional range of metrical and stanzaic forms.[33] But he presumably used his working-notebooks or loose sheets of

[29] *Letters*, V.174.
[30] Though she placed it below *Marmion* even so: *Biography*, 39n.
[31] Markings in Hardy's copy of *The Golden Treasury* (DCM) show that at some point he also read carefully through the remainder of the volume.
[32] *Life*, 478.
[33] See the excellent discussion of this topic in Dennis Taylor, *Hardy's Metres and Victorian Prosody* (Oxford: Clarendon Press, 1988).

paper for his now all but vanished attempts at actual poems,[34] and since it was in 1865, the year of beginning 'Studies, Specimens &c.', that he wrote out an elaborate listing of 'Kindred sounds' on some blank leaves at the end of Walker's *Rhyming Dictionary*,[35] it seems clear that he was conducting his specifically prosodic experiments elsewhere. In 'Studies, Specimens &c.', at any rate, both the 'studies' and the 'specimens' remain essentially lexical in character, as if directed towards the development of a personal poetic language resourceful enough to generate the ingredients of future but as yet unimagined poems.

That Hardy saw himself as pursuing some such steadily incremental programme—not so much thrusting towards urgent self-expression as setting himself deliberately to acquire, apprentice-like, the verbal equipment of his prospective trade—is strongly suggested by the way in which the quotations in the notebook are increasingly interspersed with variations and experiments of his own. Especially remarkable in this respect are those sections—sometimes headed 'Con' or 'concoc', for 'concoction'—in which what appears to be a randomly chosen passage from the Old Testament (e.g. Ezekiel, at 51.4–52.17) or the Book of Common Prayer (72.1–14) is worked over, phrase by phrase, in such a way as to produce new variations on the original words, to deploy both originals and variations within wholly new contexts, and even, it sometimes seems (e.g. Habakkuk, at 70.12–71.19), to attempt by a process of associative accretion to move towards the evolution of something vaguely resembling an independent prose-poem—typically, and despite the biblical starting-point, a poem of love or sexual desire.

It is curious to see Hardy, here and elsewhere in the notebook, deliberately generating such imagery from verse or prose passages of a decidedly non-erotic character.[36] It was magnanimous despair alone that led the editors to discover, in a late chapter of Thomas Rickman's classic work of architectural history, *An Attempt to*

---

[34] For the scanty surviving evidence of such experimentation see Richard L. Purdy, *Thomas Hardy: A Bibliographical Study* (1954; Oxford: at the Clarendon Press, 1968), facing 242, and *Biography*, 89.

[35] The date '1865' in TH's hand appears at the foot of one of these pages, and while it was perhaps a later addition its authenticity seems confirmed by the appearance of the same date, accompanied by the Westbourne Park Villas address, on the volume's half-title (DCM).

[36] The issues touched upon in this and the following paragraph are more fully explored in Pamela Dalziel's 'Hardy's Sexual Evasions: The Evidence of the "Studies, Specimens &c." Notebook', *Victorian Poetry*, 31 (1993), 143–55.

*Discriminate the Styles of Architecture in England,* the improbable stimuli ('fine hollow mouldings', 'sweep of mouldings', 'a plain return', etc.) for Hardy's 'fine-drawn kisses', 'sweep of lip', 'coming & returning of breast', etc. (62.16–17, 62.17, 63.5–6). In turning for a starting point to that career he was hoping to abandon, Hardy was no doubt presenting a deliberate challenge to his transformative powers—as when eschewing the lushness of such biblical texts as the Song of Solomon in favour of the relative aridity of Habakkuk and Ezekiel—but the sheer arbitrariness and even perversity of such choices seems strangely of a piece with the pervasive indirection and even coyness of his handling of sexual language throughout the 'Studies, Specimens &c.' notebook. In a passage of his own composition, for example, he feels for some reason obliged to render 'sweet ache of neck, lip, soul' as 'sweet ache of n—k, l–p, s—l' (60.2–3), and in a number of comparable situations he has discreet recourse to the shorthand he had recently been learning, apparently with a view to obtaining work of some journalistic sort.[37]

Although shorthand is not used extensively in the notebook, it does occur with some frequency as a replacement for direct or indirect references to parts of the body, to sexual acts, or to sexual desire. The word 'love', it is true, appears often enough for brevity to figure as one of the justifications for its being so regularly rendered in shorthand, but some form of inhibition or embarrassment—operative even in so private a document—seems clearly to be involved in the substitution of shorthand symbols for 'went to bed to her' in an early quotation from *Pericles*, 'he went to bed to her very description' (7.18), and for the similar concealment of 'breasts' itself in 'her breasts two heaving/snowy young/new mushrooms with lady birds set on their crowns, that never have seen the sun' (38.12–14), an untypically extravagant flight of Hardy's own that was apparently stimulated by the provocative example of Burns. Towards the end of the notebook the shorthand symbol for 'imitate' appears alongside a number of quoted passages, arguably for brevity's and simplicity's sake but perhaps indicative once more of a certain uneasiness or sense of guilt on Hardy's part.[38]

---

[37] *Letters*, I.5; Hardy's shorthand is based primarily on John Henry Cooke's *Taylor's System of Stenography, or Short-Hand Writing* (London: Simpkin, Marshall, 1856); his own copy (DCM) is annotated 'The best system'.

[38] Many years later he was to offer some distinctly cynical advice as to the prudentiality of a young poet's beginning his career with '*imitative* poetry, adopting the manner and views of any recent poet': *Letters*, V.345.

The exhortation itself, however, is significant of that progression from a self-educative to an actively creative agenda which is traceable throughout 'Studies, Specimens &c.' and particularly evident in its final pages, with their analytical comments, directive memoranda, and glances forward to the early fiction. It is in the published prose works of the early 1870s that the results of the 'Studies, Specimens &c.' project are to be most immediately looked for—indistinguishable though they may sometimes be from the products of his other reading and of his continuing use (specifically recorded within his own copy) of Nuttall's *Standard Pronouncing Dictionary*[39]—but the continuing importance of the notebook and of the work it represented emerges clearly enough from the verse he published from 1898 onwards. Especially in poems identified as having originated in the years between 1865 and 1870 words and phrases once quoted from other poets are abundantly present—compare, for example, the 'ruined hues' of the first line of 'Amabel'[40] with 39.6 and 9.3 of the notebook—and even Hardy's own inventions and variations of that early period occasionally recur, the 'clanging town' of 'From Her in the Country',[41] for instance, strongly recalling the notebook's 'clanging thunder' (83.2) and 'the hot ado of fevered hopes' of 'Revulsion'[42] harking directly back to 'the hot ado of blushes' (60.7).[43] Earlier, in the prose, another such experiment, 'brows in slurs' (38.10), had resurfaced in *The Hand of Ethelberta* as 'The arch of the brows—like a slur in music',[44] and Hardy's cherished mushroom imagery—present at 22.14–15 as well as in the celebration of female beauty already cited—was applied in the manuscript of *Far from the Madding Crowd* to the hands of Fanny Robin's dead child, only to be omitted from the published text at the insistence (it would appear) of Leslie Stephen.[45]

Future analysis of the notebook and of its relationship to the published prose and verse will doubtless reveal further interrelationships of both a direct and indirect kind—and not only in the form of the

[39] Opposite the title-page of his own copy (DCM) Hardy has written his name, the date 1865, and, at a later date, the note 'Used by T.H. when writing "Far from the Madding Crowd." '

[40] First published in 1898 but variously dated 1865 or 1866.

[41] First published in 1909 but dated 1866.

[42] First published in 1898 but dated from Westbourne Park Villas.

[43] Compare also the 'fabric fair' of 'Ditty (E. L. G.)', first published in *Wessex Poems* but dated 1870, with 'delicate fabric of thine eye, skin, cheek' (66.7–8).

[44] Wessex Edn. 288; the paragraph containing the phrase is absent from the serial but present in the 1st edn.

[45] *Biography*, 160.

sometimes obtrusively introduced quotations, allusions, and chapter epigraphs of the early novels: such a connection perhaps exists, for example, between Hardy's early interest in *Love's Labour's Lost* (79.7–82.9) and his incorporation of the play into the action of *A Laodicean* thirteen or fourteen years later.[46] It may be unreasonable, however, to expect an especially rich trawl of such instances. 'Studies, Specimens &c.' is essentially a poetry notebook, and—apart from a very few manuscript fragments, one or two poems printed in works of fiction, and the apparently eccentric 'Fire at Tranter Sweatley's'—nothing else survives to show or suggest what Hardy's early attempts at verse were like, or to fill in the thirty-year gap between 1868 and the 1898 publication of *Wessex Poems*. What is above all important about the notebook is precisely the uniqueness— and remarkable specificity—of its witness to a stage of Hardy's development which would otherwise remain almost completely mysterious. And to identify that stage as marked, especially in its and the notebook's earlier phases, by naïvety, educational deprivation, and painful autodidactic effort is to recognize yet again how self-created Hardy was, what extraordinary distances he had to travel, and with what rapidity and completeness he put his awkward apprenticeship behind him and moved into the full stride of his professional career.

[46] Wessex Edn. 262–5.

# Bibliographical Description

THE notebook, measuring 15.6 by 9.6 cm., is bound in stiff boards covered in black leather stamped with a straight-grain morocco pattern within a decorative border. The spine is wrapped in black cloth tape, apparently a repair carried out by Hardy himself. The first leaf of the notebook's first gathering has been pasted down to form the front endpaper, with the second leaf constituting the front free-endpaper; a sheet of orange pink surface paper has been pasted over the front endpaper and the recto of the front free-endpaper. The final leaf of the final gathering has been pasted down to form the rear endpaper.

The notebook comprises five sewn gatherings, the first two of twelve leaves each, the third of fourteen leaves, and the final two again of twelve leaves each. The first gathering is complete, its first and second leaves serving as endpapers; in the second gathering the final leaf has been torn away or become detached; the third gathering is complete; in the fourth gathering the final seven leaves have been cut away; in the fifth gathering all leaves have been cut away except the fifth, sixth, and twelfth (the rear endpaper) and a single leaf has been glued in between the stubs of the first and second leaves. Although the paper of this inserted leaf is consistent with that of the remainder of the notebook, the presence of an erased pencil page number in its upper right-hand corner suggests that it was originally part of another notebook, presumably destroyed by Hardy himself. With this exception the leaves are not foliated.

All leaves are identical in size with the cover of the notebook and ruled with blue lines, nineteen per page at 7.5-mm. intervals. The top margins vary from 14 to 16 mm., the bottom margins from 9.5 to 11.5 mm. The paper, dark cream in colour, has artificially imposed chain lines but no watermarks and varies in thickness from 0.11 to 0.12 mm.

# Editorial Procedures

THE basic principle of the edition is that of a typographical 'facsimile'. Although no attempt has been made to reproduce precisely (i.e. photographically) the actual appearance of the original, its page divisions and line-by-line layout are exactly followed and Hardy's interlineations shown in place. The spellings and abbreviations (e.g. 'wh' for 'which') of the edition are also those of the original, as is the punctuation, including all ellipsis marks. Those deletions which Hardy made by striking through or overscoring remain in the text with a horizontal line drawn through the word or word-fragment in question, and his uses of shorthand and other signs and diagrams are reproduced, graphically, as and where they occur in the notebook itself. Such signs include ∴ to mean 'therefore', = to introduce definitions and, occasionally, variations, and parenthesized underlining ͜ within quotations to register the absence of italicization in the source. No symbols have been editorially introduced other than angle brackets ⟨ ⟩, used to record doubtful readings of pencil erasures (see the next paragraph), and the arbitrary §§§§, used on one occasion only to register the presence of some illegible shorthand deleted by overscoring.

Some minor standardizations of layout have, however, been introduced in the interests of making the notebook easier to use and quote. The original document is unpaginated and unfoliated, but both page and folio numbers have been supplied at the top of each page and line numbers provided in the right margins. Spacing (as between words and lines) has been regularized, and slight anticipatory slips of the pen within an individual word (e.g. 4.6 'misbegotten', where Hardy first wrote 'mib', then altered the 'b' to an 's') are neither shown in place nor recorded in the 'Textual Notes'; the latter do, however, record such self-corrections as added words or punctuation marks and superimpositions of one punctuation mark upon another. The edition makes no typographical distinction between ink and pencil inscriptions, but the original is almost entirely in ink and all uses of pencil are recorded in the 'Textual Notes'. All erasures, whether of ink or pencil, are also recorded in the 'Textual Notes', and recoverable erasures (other than pencil erasures that have simply been inked over) are shown in place in the edited text against a shaded background, thus: publishers hack. Because Hardy's pencil erasures have proved to be of considerable interest in this particular document, at the two points (84.10–17, 89.1–3 *inv.*) where they chiefly occur angle brackets have been employed both to acknowledge the tentativeness of certain readings and to indicate, by their enclosure of blank space, the extent of the erased entries that have eluded recovery, thus: Talk to ⟨Mac⟩ Craik ⟨          ⟩. All but one of the erased pencillings on the final leaf appear upside down in the original document, Hardy having evidently inscribed them with the notebook turned back to front; this inversion has been preserved in the present edition, the portion of the text involved being numbered downward from the top of the page when inverted. In the Annotations and Textual Notes cross-references to the inverted material are identified by the addition of '*inverted*' or '*inv.*'.

Hardy's inscriptions in the notebook conform in general to the pattern he indicated (almost certainly at a later date) on the verso of the front free-endpaper, quotations copied down from other authors being followed by parentheses containing his own 'Explanatory' notes and 'Additions'—in practice, definitions, variations, experiments, and comments of every sort. The pattern is not consistently maintained—parentheses are sometimes missing, for instance, experiments and personal word-lists separately set out—but the distinction is always sufficiently clear between what is being quoted and what supplied by Hardy himself, and any word or phrase not commented upon in the 'Annotations' will have been adjudged by the editors to fall within the latter category. The 'Annotations' do, however, explicate Hardy's shorthand symbols wherever they occur and comment upon any references (e.g. of a biographical character) that lie outside the contexts provided by the notebook itself.

In identifying the source of a quotation the editors have always sought to trace, whenever possible, the edition and even the actual copy of the edition that Hardy was probably using and the particular occurrence of the quoted word or phrase he seems most likely to have encountered just prior to the moment of inscription—although other occurrences (particularly of single words) may well occur elsewhere within the same work or within other works by the same author. Differences in the textual situation as between one author and another or one work and another have necessarily affected the format of the identifications, and when a specific edition cannot be

confidently identified or when an identified edition (e.g. the multi-
volume Shakespeare Hardy owned in the 1860s) imposes a non-
standard form of citation, the entry in the 'Annotations' will provide
an alternative or supplementary reference to a readily available standard edition. The first quotation or group of quotations from a particular author and work is always preceded by a headnote giving full
bibliographical details of the relevant editions; whenever Hardy
quotes again from the same source the bibliographical information is
not repeated but can be located either by means of the cross-references supplied or by consulting the index, where initial bibliographical entries are shown in bold. When all quotations within a group
are from a single work (e.g. *In Memoriam*), the title of that work is
given only in the headnote; when, however, a group includes quotations from different constituents of a collective work (e.g. the separate
poems included in *The Golden Treasury*), the individual title is given in
each entry.

The lemmata in both the 'Annotations' and 'Textual Notes' are
cued by page and line number to the edited text, but the former
differ from the latter in reproducing only the verbal forms of that
text as distinct from such features as underlining, double underlining,
and shading. Discrepancies in wording between a given quotation
and its probable source are recorded in the 'Annotations' at the end
of the relevant identification, but discrepancies in punctuation and
spelling (apart from dialect spellings in William Barnes's poems) are
not so recorded, nor are words that Hardy himself omitted from a
quotation by means of an ellipsis. Whenever the probable source is
a surviving volume from Hardy's library and the quoted word
or phrase is found to have been marked there in some fashion,
an appropriate note (e.g. 'underlined') is added to the identification;
the note 'footnoted' is added whenever the quoted word or
phrase is defined or explicated in a footnote to the probable
source.

Unless otherwise indicated, cross-references throughout the edition
are always internal, directing attention to another section of the editorial apparatus (e.g. 'see Introduction, xii'), to specific lines of the
edited text (e.g. 'see 13.1'), or, using 'n.' for 'note', to a particular
annotation (e.g. 'see 13.1 n.').

To facilitate use of the edition by scholars with a general interest
in Hardy's reading as well as by those with specific interests in individual works the index engages in some duplication of information,

supplying page references to the Notebook itself both inclusively, for each individual author, and analytically, for each individually titled work by each author.

T. Hardy

16 Westbourne Park Villas

1865.

Thomas Hardy.

      Bockhampton

         Dorchester '67

---

  Explanatory (      ), additional exp. (−     )                 5

  Additions [∴     ]

      except Biblic:

    wh. are all add. exc "———"

To be <u>destroyed</u>                                        (Pri:)

Studies, Specimens &c.
———————————┼┼
1865 <u>Notes.</u>

Shakesp.

It is I                          5

That all the abhorred things o' the earth <u>do mend</u>

<u>By being worse than they</u>. /

Nor did he <u>soil the fact</u> with cowardice /

The hour

Labouring for nine /                          10

If after <u>two days' shine</u>, Athens contain thee /

For his occasions might have <u>woo'd me</u> first

(i.e, he might h. asked me first)


Wordsworth.

These all <u>wear out</u> of me (thought of them              15

goes from me) / <u>Square with</u> my desire /

its <u>faint undersong</u> / <u>flapping</u> / <u>jibe</u> / <u>rancour</u> /

tarn = mere = lake / strains <u>of rapture</u> /

the <u>more than</u> reasoning mind / <u>mutable</u> /

Scott:  the <u>lated</u> peasant = <u>belated</u> — /

. . <u>signs</u> the <u>frequent</u> cross //

By:  <u>grow native</u> of the soil [also Spen:]

<u>so many a</u> <u>meaner</u> crest / sable shore //

Sc: O'er <u>moss</u> & <u>moor</u> o'er <u>holt</u> & <u>hill</u> / with      5

<u>reverted</u> eye = eye turned behind / <u>misbegotten</u> /

<u>yawning rifts</u> / <u>tangled</u> thorn / rede =

advice / to rede = to advise / <u>shagged with</u>

thorn / <u>to speed</u> = to push on / <u>selle</u> = saddle

(also by Spenser) / to hear her love the loved     10

one tell //

Spenser:  sunny day / <u>half loth</u> / middest /

<u>dispread</u> / mis-diet / to hurlten / <u>aiding</u> = help

<u>to neighbour</u> / <u>meeter</u> / <u>unweeting</u> = unknowing /

Shakes:  <u>freshes</u> = springs of water / <u>rootedly</u> = thorou$^y$
                    [sing]
Will you <u>troll</u>ₐ the <u>catch</u> you taught me but     16

<u>while-ere</u>? / <u>ladykin</u> = a little lady /

Sp:  Men into stones therewith he c$^d$ transmew

And stones to dust, & dust to nought at all. /

The iron rowels into <u>frothy foam</u> he bit /

<u>captived</u> = captivated / thereto said he /

<u>chase away</u> sleep / <u>hoped</u> victory /

I <u>no whit</u> <u>reck</u> / <u>odds</u> / <u>doughty</u> tourna-

ment / <u>oriental</u> gate of heaven / <u>sunbright</u>          5

arms / <u>ruth</u> / her darksome <u>mew</u> =

prison / <u>where when</u> she came / wretched

<u>thralls</u> = slaves / <u>Ind</u> / looking <u>lovely</u> /

<u>ransack'd</u> chastity / <u>piteous</u> maiden /

<u>salvage</u> / are <u>won</u> [to] pity & <u>unwonted</u>          10
                    with

ruth / an ivy <u>twine</u> / Cybele's <u>frantic</u>

<u>rites</u> / dryadés =          hamadˢ =

naiadés / <u>timely</u> / <u>sturdy</u> courage / <u>behest</u> /

to <u>weet</u> of news = to know of n. / <u>Araby</u> = . . bia /

The <u>lesser</u> pangs can bear who hath en-          15

dured the <u>chief</u> / <u>new breath'd</u> / leasing

= lying / with foul words <u>tempering</u> fair /

when him <u>list</u> / <u>transmew</u> /

<u>Wordsw</u>.

fulgent / <u>trim</u> array / what <u>boots</u> it /

<u>stress</u> / <u>bedimming</u> / <u>sepulchral</u> / sky

<u>muffled</u> in clouds / <u>imaging</u> / the

<u>wish'd-for</u> / to <u>brood</u> / <u>chaplet</u> = wreath          5

one <u>after</u> one / one may be used = I /


Sir W. S. Marmion

c. 5 & 6.

aright / manned = boldened / strook /

hostel / chapelle / selle = saddle /                    10

wingèd / vext / donned / rack, wrack /

dank / mellowing / urn = tomb / to wake =

to waken / kindly / laggard / mimosa =

sensitive plant / cap of maintenance, =

i.e. of state, dignity / meet time /                    15

the steep / the eddy / the mystic sense = meaning /

lordly / laced = interlaced / cumber /

had happed / Highland broadsword,

targe & plaid / sable pines / trode /

whin = furze / breezes thin / I ween /

vassal-rank = row of vassals / pavillion

= tent / the ruddy lion <u>ramped</u> in gold /

the whilst / leagured / 'gainst / larum /

inveighs ag$^{st}$ / riven / umbered = browned /        5

corslet =                    / paly / whilome /

matchless / whilere = erewhile / Toledo

blade / a minstrel's malison

gibber / Wh of you all, touched his

harp with that dying <u>fall</u> / the torrent        10

....... say have ~~yel~~ ye lost each wild maj$^{c}$

<u>close,</u> / that erst the choir of bards or

Druids <u>flung</u>? / trumpet-jubilee. / tinct,

tincture / like apprehension's hurried

glow / sorrow's livery / yare = ready /        15


Shakes: Praises wh are paid as

debts & not as given / Paragon to

all reports / ... that he ꝏ ɪ. ꝗ ɪ ⱴ very descrip$^{n}$ /

Varˢ. it irks me / crimson sheen /

flaccid / tense / better hand = right h. /

nether / réflex = reflection / parlance

athwart / sheeny / rivage / marge /

vary- (various) ~~mar~~ coverture / sere /     5

pleasance / whilome / glean'd (gather'd /

anon / moil /


Gol. Trea:  palm / decore = decorate /

diadem of pearl / frisk / <u>blushing</u>

beams / did once thy heart <u>surprise</u> /     10

<u>pipe</u> all day / sunning / <u>tune</u>

this merry lay / purely white / ivybuds /

<u>deck</u> thyself in <u>fairest guise</u> / the

clouds with <u>orient gold</u> <u>spangle</u> their

blue / stud / honey breath / Time's     15

best jewel / melodious birds sing

madrigals / falls (water) / carol

enjoy & miss her / teeming autumn

big with rich increase / my rose, thou .. /

three summer's pride (3 years' leaves) /

<u>sweet</u> hue / I <u>do</u> love thee / sweets /

dear joy (thee)   twines (of hair) /

sapphires set in snow / blushing cloud //                    5

sting / your furious <u>chiding</u> stay /

<u>fell</u> hand / alack / bare / freezings

have I felt / beweep / bootless /

sullen earth / Ah, yet doth beauty

like a dial hand, steal from his                              10

figure & no pace perceived / <u>paint</u>

the sable skies / rouse / career =

path / wont / chase hence / sworn

(ordered) / tarry / makes vanish / reels

shun / outworn buried age / buried                           15

age / razed /confounded = ruined /

o'ersways / plea / battering days /

prime / [such] spoil of beauty / craggy

mountains / kirtle / nimble / hic /

defy / folks / crowned (finished) / truest

mettle / vary / tend = attend upon / bid /

fleeting / old December / mute /

featured like / that man's scope /

scorn to ... / ranged = wandered / All                    5

frailties that besiege all kinds of

blood / <u>sum</u> of good / prove me = try m. /

selfsame / aye / happed / haply /

her lips are like two <u>budded</u> roses

whom <u>ranks</u> of lilies <u>neighbour</u>                 10

<u>nigh</u> / <u>centres</u> of delight / orbs /

feed perfection = keep perfect what

is already so / with orient pearl, with

sapphire blue with marble white, with

ruby red her body every way is fed                         15

yet soft in touch & sweet in view /

nymphs / calm / <u>darling</u> buds / every

fair from fair sometimes declines /

beauty making beautiful / beauty's best /

passing fair / Love whose month is

ever May / velvet leaves / fondle /

bemoan / chidden / dimm'd / brand /

mischanced / apt to entice / imprisoned

(abstractions in material forms) /                                5

moulds = makes / <u>muse</u> not / spied /

<u>wasted</u> time (old) / blazon (display)

lack / prefiguring / <u>divining</u> eyes /

unmeet = unfit / deny himself for

[to be] Jove / intent / travail / assays /          10

amiss / riot / sometime / 'gan /

   Shelley:  the blast = wind / strip me stark /

bare = bore / beamless & pallid / circling sea /

silentness / topmost / its sails were flagging /

tameless resolve / linked remembrance /          15

methought / when low winds attune the

midnight pines / infold = fold / tranced /

wildering / joyance / darkness was piled /

wove a shade / did flee /

Byron:  harp ... c$^d$ <u>string</u> (play)    albeit (2 syl)

fellest / whereon = on wh /

   Shakes:  cram their words into mine

ears / rate (for consider) / weighed between

= hesitated between / escape = not do /                    5

tilth = culture, tillage / nimble lungs =

susceptibility / hest = behest / skill-less /

totters / marmozet = a small monkey /

    Shell:  mailed against / he inly weets /

swart = swarthy / countered = encountered /              10

    Scott:  glozed upon = fawned, flattered /

On the deck ...... the abbess of St Hilda placed

= being placed / heirs = succeeds / when

cloyed each wish / begirdled / and dew

the woods / Staindrop .... <u>whom</u> .. salutes /              15

pouring a lay / dimwood / Knitting as

with a moral band thy native legends

with thy land / in the dawning seen /

spires = points / grisly = frightful /

in his despite = in spite of h. / pull'd

the wilding spray & brambles / tuck

of drum / I read you for a bold dragoon =

guess, think / teach a tale = tell a t. /

tale of eld / spell = (guess) / ban dog (large                5

dog, mastiff / submiss(ve) / when eve

his oaks embrowned / nor mirth nor wine

c$^d$ e'er one wrinkled knot untwine / to

wot so well (to imagine s. w)    aught of rich

and rare / I hold my wont / to blench                        10

(shrink)    our hardiest venture / spial (a spy)

sally port (door of exit) / fair (good / roundelay

(3 syl) / I trow (imagine) / some early love

shaft grazed his heart / centred in /Allan-

a-Dale was ne'er belted a knight / to lodge                  15

the deer (discover his retreat)) / to pitch both

toil and net / garth (yard) / thy desperate

quest (search) / azure pencilled flower /

festal time / wilding (an apple t. not grafted,

also adj:) /                                                 20 and down its clustered stores to hail (hail down &c)

on upland fades.. / this helpless fair /

the tale goes   a ring of rugged kerne /

in this bound (limit) / prone / reared

(built) / taxing his fancy / dally not (                          5

waste no time) / prore = prow / according

(agreeing) / heathery / bold burst ... /

lave / emprise (enterp.)   the guardian

in her bosom chid / more loud & louder /

pipe music / amain = with force / foreshow          10

to ban / doom him wrath & woe /

serest (yellowest) / font (fountain) / bristles /

　　　Shak:  twink (twinkle) / brims

(edges of lakes &c also) marges / thyself

dost air / scarf / opposing (opposite) /               15

　　　Sc:  tell, guess, spell, bode, read, trace /

troth (truth) / paled in (bounded) / months

had scantly flown / stolen-wise / well-

a-day (alas!) / their date was fled / poured

the lay ) wight / coined badge of empery )

Jean I.  It was a happy thing to sit

so near (nor) mar his reverie / like roses

blown / in loving wise / bide / blue bergs /

navigate the moon-led main / vagrant                    5

fancy fraught / my sometime pride /

my heart within (within m. h. / wis, (know)

wist (knew) / who find not aught thereto

akin / to brim (overflow) / whelmed

(overwhelmed)   albeit / lithe & tall /              10

tendance / the little trembling word

took flight; she answered, No. / forecasting

(foreseeing)   a quest = (a searching)

waxing life (increasing age) / He would

fain that life w$^d$ at a stand remain,                 15

eternally / let fall (tell) / flusheth the

rise (knoll) with her purple favour

(ornament) / to prank (adorn showily)

beck (small brook) / westering (going west)

[southing, northing: Chaucer]                        20

Shak:  so he (so that he)

 Shell:  utmost (most distant)   a might

of human thought / cradled in that

night / in woven passions mailed / our

mingling spirits brooded / outspring (spring    5

out) / scare / smiles to steep your hearts in

balm / a film then overcast my sense with

dimness / kingly (fine, noble)   giddy turret /

idle winds / spire, far lessening in the sky /

flower-inwoven crowns / token flowers /    10

to lead a dance (to d.) / a rainbow, braided /

 Skak:  tristful / I am not in the roll

of common men (rank of c. m) / hold

me pace (keep up with me) / gelding the

opposed continent / honey .. whereof a    15

little more than a little is by much too

much / aweary

 Sc:  seems as (it seems as) / at this tide /

the rites of spousal / benison / port (stature)

Orcades (Orkneys)

She: that ill might none betide him (that

no ill mᵗ b. him) / the day whereon /

an aerial hymn / disk of the broad earth /

blinding beams of morning /       5

Col: the gentle dew-fall : terms wh we

trundle smoothly o'er our tongues : aslant :

a three years child : may'st (thou may'st)

 She: ken / shall cull from thought / mists

of night entwining their dim woof / moveless /  10

infinite throng (many) / speechless (silent)

Earth when she smiles in the embrace of
     look &
Autumn / every﹀ mind fed on her form /

the dusky main (sea at night) / weaving

swift language from impassioned themes /   15

by the shrieks of their own terror driven /

artillery's bolt (cannon shot) / the dead & the

alive / term (end, point, top, bottom, close)

I heard her musical pants.

with mountain flowers dispread / the

baffled heart / blasts : strewed strangest

sounds : the sickness of a deep & speechless

swoon of joy : the thick ties of her soft hair :

gentle might / those who grow together cannot        5

choose but love : our talk befel of the

late ruin : wh made its floor (formed)

By: laying all things prone (low) / rear

their leaves / hiving wisdom : ~~mast~~

irony, that master-spell : compels (brings)        10

   Sha:  doff : unknit this churlish

knot of all-abhorred war : move in

that obedient orb again : a portent

(omen) : broached : unborn time (coming t)

outdare : sufferances borne : to forge        15

(to make) : impaint : trimmed up your

praises with a princely tongue : vaunting

enemies : ill weav'd ambition, how

much art thou shrunk : from the

orient to the drooping west : apter :

the ragged'st hour that time & spite dare

bring : lean (rest on) : presurmise : as

if he had writ "man" ever since his father

was a bachelor :                                                  5

   <u>By</u>:  a harmless wile : to fleet along :

   loss or̗ guerdon : I have not flatter'd its

[the world's] rank breath : bowed a patient

knee : coined my cheek to smiles :

respire (live) : is skilful to diffuse :                          10

over-weening phantasies (overween, to think

too fondly, highly) : I've taught me other

tongues : and light the laurels on a loftier

head (may the l. light on &c)

   <u>Mi</u>:  tree whose mortal <u>taste</u> : <u>secret</u>            15

top : the deep <u>tract</u> of Hell : <u>seduced</u>

them to that <u>foul</u> revolt : <u>baleful</u> eyes :

<u>utmost</u> pole : <u>sights</u> of woe (scenes of w)

urges (presses, impends)   the <u>potent</u> victor :

can else inflict (besides) : outward lustre :

Swin:  for all you are, you may see bitter

days : all will die of you : the dull blood

beats at my face & blinds me : sharp joy :

some river flower that breathes against the                    5

stream like a swooned swimmer's mouth :

bound about with flesh : at naked ebb :

dead lute strain : have the better of us : shut

fast on it : the least pain plucks them back

the great fight jarred and joined : I cᵈ                         10

see by fits, some : my heart swelled out

with thirst :

Sha:  lean on your health (other lives) :

would lift him where most trade of danger

ranged : this stiff-borne action : brought                     15

forth (ended in) : the gain proposed choked

the respect of likely peril feared : wrought

out life (achieved our safety) : up (ready)

this present grief had wiped it from my mind

the aptest way : counter (against) : all you

that kiss my lady peace at home : baying him

at the heels : but rather show awhile

like fearful war, to <u>diet</u> <u>rank</u> minds

sick of happˢ ; & <u>purge</u> the obstructⁿˢ wh                    5

begin to stop our very veins of life : <u>torrent</u>

of occasion : the <u>summary</u> of all our

griefs : any branch of it (part) : newly

(lately)   concurring (agreeing) : to seal : the

edge of ... (chief point of ) : bruises :                    10

  Word:  Sad vacuities : bourn (bound of

journey) : crazing care : nod : swelling :

thrown between (lying bet.:)   upstayed (supportᵈ⁾

mists, suspended on the expiring gale : moveless :

the beams of evenᵍ slipping soft between :                    15

lengthens (continues to extend out) : dewy lights :

dilated :

  By:  and on the curl <u>hangs</u> pausing (wave) :

infant (little) : gird : to understand, not feel.

thy <u>lyric flow</u> (inversion of n. & ad.)

    <u>Recoll</u>:  hussy : sniff (smell)

the breaking day : clinking off :

glowed & stared : cricket : traps

quite the dand(y) wizen : like               5

a long dog : looby : crony :

nammut : poor body : jogging on

crisp : blinking : tittering : prim

wabble : rose-red :

    <u>Burns</u>:  flaunting : sunward        10

nature sickened : silk-saft

    Gol T.  that <u>wave</u> hot youth <u>to</u> —

To <u>cease upon</u> the midnight

    <u>Inv</u>:  smoothy soft as new-spring

mushroom crowns : eye so wondrous blue :     15

    Shak — <u>niggard</u> of question : edge [on] :

colour — (give its nature to)   <u>smart</u> lash :

    shock : awry : as lief : cope with

loth : mich (slink) : tax him home :

bound to [hence e.g. bound <u>for</u> pleasure—&c]
                      (win)
to buy out [or to buy∧ e.g. buy a kiss with truth]

bow [the knee] : <u>wring</u> your heart :

---

Isa:  'Thy tacklings are loosed.' — works                5

sweetness, she works delight — 'trodden down'

— 'that fly as a cloud'


By.  'the waves <u>bound</u> beneath me' — '<u>strew</u>

<u>the gale</u>' 'Still must I <u>on</u>' — 'again I

<u>seize</u> the theme' — 'the last <u>sands</u> of life —      10

'so it' (so that it) — nor below can love

(& who cannot love below) — 'he drooped'

'woos us' (attracts us) 'where <u>rose</u> the mountˢ

'tire of' 'chiefless caṣtles'

  <u>Mem</u>:  the terminⁿ -<u>less</u>; & the comp            15

& sup. -<u>er</u> & -<u>est</u>, also the -<u>er</u> of cause.

    Shak:  'say No' (refuse) 'cast my love'

'I chid hence' [Mem: wish a wish — think

a thought &c : — particip$^s$ in -ed & -ing] —

'to relish a love song' — 'I w$^d$ have had

them writ more movingly' — 'And Silvia

<u>shews</u> Julia but a swarthy Ethiope' (compared                    5

with J. is but &c) 'aiming at' (striving for)

'as <u>far from</u> fraud' (as free from) — 'a <u>hard</u>

opinion'

   <u>Bur</u> — scrimply (fr. to scrimp) — the

sun had <u>closed</u> the winter day — 'peer it'                      10

(equal it)  '<u>drew</u> my gazing wonder' [∴ drew

my g.] — and hermit Ayr staw through his

woods —


   [<u>belted</u> by (surrounded by) — <u>mounting</u>

star]                                                                 15

<u>Wor</u>: wreaths of smoke <u>sent</u> up — affect$^{ns}$

gently <u>lead</u> us on

In Mem ₍₇₉₎  closed grave doubts (ended) —

~~these grave~~ slender shade of doubt —

vassal unto love — loosens from (leaves)

— the schools — glance from (reflect from)

— breaks about the dappled pools — the                    5
        be with me when     is low
fancy's tenderest eddy —ᴧ my lightᴧ (hope)

— when my faith is dry — to point (-to)

— vileness — and I be lessened in his

love : love reflects the thing beloved —

topmost froth — dash'd with —                              10

sunder'd — heats of youth — preach —

slope through darkness up to God —

lame hands — scarped cliff — roll'd

the psalm — crypt ‑  she sighs amid

her narrow days — tease her — change                       15

replies (ex-)   the circle of the wise —

vaster — a higher height, a deeper deep

to round (to go round) — divinely gifted

man — invidious bar — the skirts of

happy chance, and breasts the blows of

circumstance & grapples with his

evil star — to mould (make) — and

shape the whisper of the throne — crowning

slope (top) — a distant dearness in the                    5

hill, a secret sweetness in the stream —

his narrower fate — I lull a fancy

trouble-tost — move thee on to (incite)

till dusk is dipt in gray — times my

breath — knows not (has nothing like)                    10

resolve the doubt — reached (-forth) —

touch it into leaf — wizard music roll —

dark bulks — a night-long Present

of the Past — treble strong — grow

to — the river's reach — the cataract                    15

flashing from the bridge — Day, who

mightst have heavéd a windless flame

beam & shade — chequerwork — lift —

sow the sky with flying boughs — thick

noon — <u>joyless</u> gray — <u>kindred with</u> (re-

lationship with)

    The world which credits what is done

    Is cold to all that might have been.

set thy face where (turn to) — take wings of        5

    <u>foresight</u> — <u>ring with</u> — snow <u>possessed</u>

    the earth — no <u>wing</u> of wind the <u>region</u>

    swept, but over all things brooding <u>slept</u> —

    the winters <u>left behind</u> (past) —

    O last regret, Regret can die!        10

<u>mixt</u> with — dropt on (threw on) —

then fancy <u>shapes</u>, as fancy can —

<u>unused</u> example from the grave — feud —

transplanted human worth, will

<u>bloom to profit</u>, otherwhere — garners in        15

(collects in) — dip down upon — <u>stays</u>

<u>thee</u> from — to <u>meet</u> their least desire —

lavish — gave him welcome — poised —

I <u>count</u> it crime — my old affection

of the tomb — stain (injure) — gorgeous —

the round of space — gray flats (levels) —

aim fair — fierce extremes — dusking —

midmost — counterchange — towering —

to rout the brood of cares — whereat                    5

(at wh place) — the books to love or hate —

(devoted to) — couch'd (lying)  to talk

them o'er — (133)

By. Ch H. C III.  sole daughter — the waters

heave — the winds lift up their voices — whither     10

(to where) — glad mine eye — the waves bound — a

steed that knows his rider — guidance — strained

mast — to quiver — rent canvass [∴ heart] — strew

the gale — still must I on — I seize the theme

and bear it with me [∴ to bear thoughts in one] — the

journeying years — harp have lost a string — heart     16

& harp .. may jar — as I have sung to sing — strain

(-music) — wean me from — so it fling forgetfulness

around me — piercing the depths of life —

so that no wonder <u>waits</u> him (remains for him) — cut

<u>to</u> his heart — <u>endurance</u> — why thought <u>seeks</u>

<u>refuge in</u> lone caves — <u>rife with</u> airy images —

<u>live a being</u> more intense — <u>mix'd with</u> thy

spirit — thy birth (life) — <u>feeling with</u>                    5
                    (darkly
thee — to think (wildly (∴ lovingly, fondly
                    holding a
regretfully, sweetly —ᴧ thought of thee sweetens

me) — o'erwrought — phantasy — yet still

<u>enough the same</u> — time cannot <u>abate</u> —

fain — he of the breast — wrung with                    10

(hurt by) — years steal fire from the mind —

   <u>Sha:</u>  to make good — our leisure

w<sup>d</sup> <u>not let us</u> hear — <u>moreover</u> —

has thou <u>sounded</u> him — on some <u>known</u>

<u>ground</u> of — <u>sift</u> him — seen in (is in)                    15

frowning brow to brow (∴ 𝟞 of lo ſ )

<u>freely</u> — add to — tendering     hush'd —

to spur — were I <u>tied to</u> run — rites (rules)
                    be
how high a <u>pitch</u> — bidᴧ (make) — a trespass

chambered with : where shame doth

harbour : the swelling difference of

your settled hate : gage (defiance) : put

we our quarrel to the will of heaven :

hack'd down                                                    5

G.T.   Mil: afford a present to the infant God

(give) : work us (make us) : the heaven

... hath took no print of the approaching light :

join to (unite with) : if such holy song

enwrap our fancy long : melt from : the                       10

tissued clouds : casts his usurped sway (spreads)

a breathéd spell (∴ silent ♪ oppose to breathed ♪ )

edged with poplar pale : dismal : unshowered

(∴ showerless) : curtained with cloudy red : the

flocking shadows pale troop to the infernal jail :            15

slips to his several grave : maze

Dry. notes that wing their heavenly ways to

mend the choirs above.

　　Mil:  their moans the vales redoubled to the
　　　　　　　　　　　　　　　　　　　　　　hills

& they to heaven :

Marv:  where it was nurst : the emulous,

or enemy : his highest plot : plead the

ancient rights in vain : comely : the

Public's skirt : parti-coloured (- ✍ ) : victory          5

his crest does plume :

Sha Rchᵈ II:  smooth his fault : wake

his peace : a foil : craft (an art)   dive into

their hearts : throw away on : to farm : to

make for (∴ ✍ )   come short : to strive with :          10

deep harmony : spent, upon : limp after :

doth the world thrust forth a vanity : to tire (grow

weary) : to rein (curb) : gaunt : the pleasure

that some fathers feed upon is my strict

fast :          15

Exc. B.I.  showed a surface of : careless

limbs ; casts a twilight of its own : determined

(well marked) : grateful resting pl : livelier joy :

brotherhood (multitude) : slackened : seated in a tract :

to wh he <u>drew</u> (withdrew) : product : dimmer :

<u>plain</u> presence (visible pres) : <u>feeling</u> (kind)

<u>liver</u> (that wh lives) : on his mind they <u>lay</u>

<u>braced</u> : <u>equipoise</u> : a being made of many

beings : n̶          <u>By</u>: <u>sheathed</u> :                    5

R<sup>d</sup> II. Sha: <u>no whit</u> lesser : to <u>sour</u> : to <u>prick</u> to

(stimulate to) : <u>seize into</u> our hands : I'll

not <u>be by</u> <u>the while</u> : <u>fall out</u> (hap<sup>n</sup>) : <u>repair</u>

<u>to</u> : [<u>break with</u> (leave)] : the king is <u>not himself</u> :

to <u>fine</u> : <u>sit</u> sore upon : <u>making hither</u> : to          10

<u>urge</u> to (represent to) : life-<u>harming</u> ($\therefore$ the harming th<sup>t</sup>)

<u>crave</u> (require) : <u>broke his staff</u> ($\therefore$ m.b. used to

mean unnerved) : prop : <u>so</u> (for so that) my :

presages : <u>draw out</u> our miles : <u>bereft</u> :

I <u>bethink</u> me :                                          15

    Inv. a clouding — : an icing — : a grounding :

a toning — : a shaping — : a curing — : a nerving — :

a leafing — : a quenching — : a matching — :

a skilling — : a manning — : a staining — : a hurting —

<u>Sc. L. of I</u>.  his mantle's fold rests on —— :

a shroud of russet <u>dropped with</u> gold :

Ettricke's western <u>fell</u> : <u>hushed</u> (closed, ended)

<u>forms of</u> life : Autumn's <u>fading realms</u> :

stain (dye, colour) : the <u>waste</u> fields : to glean :                5

the Seer : <u>heaved on</u> the beach a softer wave :

<u>symphony</u> : <u>festal</u> day : <u>descant</u> : <u>high</u> right

is ours (full r.) : to <u>charm from</u> (win away from)

the <u>summons</u> of .. : the eagle proud will <u>poise</u>

<u>him on</u> Ben-Cailliach's cloud : <u>to mate</u>                10

the melody of thy voice : mocks (imitates) :

<u>mix with</u> Beauty's dream : wake maid

of Lorn, the moments fly wh <u>yet</u> that maiden-

name <u>allow</u> : Fear, thy bosom's fluttering

<u>guest</u> : <u>tamed</u> the Minstrel's pride had been :                15

not upon her cheek <u>awoke</u> the glow of pride :

their tenderest numbers : beauty's <u>proudest</u>

<u>pitch</u> of power : enhance : for further

<u>vouches not</u> my lay : <u>a space</u> apart :

cloistered [hidden] : her nursling : in

finished loveliness : where thwarting tides

with mingled roar part thy swarth hills

from Morvern's shore : each [tower] on its

own dark cape reclined : o'erawes (stands      5

above) : engaging with (at war w.) : given

to fame : flung his task aside & claimed

this morn for holy-tide : her hurrying hand :

sum thine Edith's wretched lot (sum up) :

the league that styled Edith : our fates      10

the same : my bosom throbbed when ~~Roland's~~
Ronald's
ᴧname came gracing Fame's heroic tale

like perfume on the summer gale : void

of energy : what requital : some lighter

love (sweethᵗ) : stoop her mast : its      15

bannered pride : to win its way against

the gale : the scud comes on : the rising

wind : at every tack : they strove with

wind & seas : the willing breeze : swept by :

streamered with silk & tricked with gold : chafes

beneath : field-ward : to the wild cadence

of the blast gave wilder minstrelsy : come

down (pass down) the darksome Sound :

so bore they on :　　　　　　　　　　　　　　　　5

　　Sha: Rd II. learn to bend their bows

against thy state : measure (to note,

read) : our confines :

　　　　　　　Dic,s

| gadder · | to emborder | sworder (solʳ) | 10 |
|---|---|---|---|
| to plush | crownet | crowd [-ykit] | |
| to tiddle | to slidder | a dallier | |
| tid (nice) | a noier (an-) | to pucker | |
| holder. | tucker = {linen shading the breast of women | | |
| dandler. | fondler | philter | 15 |

live in clover :

Spen. Epith:  my truest turtle-dove :

crystal-bright : ye lightfoot maids :

the birds' love-learned song : [goodliness] :

dimmed by : daughters of delight [love,

joy, day, morning, sunset, June, roses                    5

lilies, emotion, snow] : [thou bosom-thriller
                                that do the
thrilling-sweet] : to tower :ₐseasons of

the year allot : ye three handmaids of

the Cyprian queen : throw between (inter-

sperse) : in seemly good array : sunshiny          10

face : sovereign praises : the pipe, the

tabor, & the trembling croud : they their

timbrels smite : portly : do attire her =

(mantle her) : a garland green : modest

eyes : adorned with beauty's grace and          15

virtue's store : hath ruddied : uncrudded :

her lively spright : garnished with

heavenly gifts of high degree : there

dwells ... constant chastity : ~~~~~~~~~~

unspotted faith & comely womanhood :

chastity's sweet bower : things uncomely :

as doth behove (as is fit) : lively notes :

the red roses flush up in her cheeks : forget

their service : eyes, ... fastened on : a coronal :                    5

fitter : slowly do the hours their numbers spend :

the Western foam : is nighing fast : plight :

odoured : quietsome : young men : secret dark

make us to wish their choking (them choked)

may in assurance reign (safety, calm)                               10

divers-feathered doves : sweet snatches of

delight : play your sports : who is the same

which (this one that)?  wrought pleasures :

[enlarge my heart to hold more love] : in lieu :

smart (pain) : till when (till that time) : to                        15

increase the count (worth) : endless — [depths &c] :

leave to sing (cease) : onc look ... wh may

let in a little thought unsound :

    By:  mar into : shot a chilliness to his
                                            heart :

a <u>jocund</u> morn : <u>skirr</u> the plain :

  <u>Bu</u>: sic talents [no maid so <u>talented</u>

<u>in</u> <u>knacks o' love</u>, <u>wiles o' love</u>] : muckle

<u>din</u> : <u>loud & lang</u> : [cheeks two tidal
           ruby           (ebbed &
lakes of ruddiest (wine), that (rose                  5
flowed)
fell    ) on alabaster shores : her brow, her

blush, her eyes, sun, moon & stars had

met in jocund unity : bevy of maids = bunch

of flowers : players saw eyes in semibreves

& brows in slurs :] constellations [as mushrooms   10

bore thro' the earth, & keep their clean-ness :
           snowy) new
her ᴧ two heaving) young mushrooms with

a̶ lady birds s̶i̶t̶t̶i̶n̶g̶ ̶o̶n̶ set on their crowns,

that never have seen the sun] <u>chuckie</u> : <u>cockie</u> :

  <u>Isai.</u> ① <u>laden with</u> [sweetˢ, ↗ &c] : a <u>lodge</u> :    15

to <u>lodge in</u> : [my] <u>fed</u> [eyes] : I will <u>ease me</u>

of : <u>turn</u> my hand <u>upon</u> thee : [when I̶] <u>consume</u>

{<u>away</u> : <u>S.S.</u> ⑤ <u>fitly</u> set : a <u>bed</u> of spices :
{with

dropping sweet smelling myrrh : set with :

overlaid : drops of the night


Sh. R II: the complexion of : I play the (I am) :

to ear, [eared with] (cultivate) : royally :

mann'd against thy entrance : send                               5

the breath of parle into his ruined ears :

[sent ✑ into her heart, his eye; sent dreams

of home into {me
           {my; sent gloom. thought athwart
                   noticed
her face as at the o'erpassing cloud the pedlar

cloaks his toys, bright display] : rained from        10

[stilled from] [still from crushed hope a ....]

lay the summer's dust with : unbegot :

the testament of : the buried hand of warlike

Gaunt : laid the sentence of dread banishᵗ on
        ⟶                                  ⟵

yon proud man, shᵈ take it off again with            15

words of sooth :

| | |
|---|---|
| 1.L.  Madam, we'll tell tales | It doth remember me the more of sorrow; |
| Q           Of sorrow or of joy? | Or if of grief, being altogether had, |
| 1L.  Of either, madam | It adds more sorrow to my want of joy: |
| Q           Of neither, girl: | For what I have, I need not to repeat       20 |
| For  if of joy, being altogether wanting | And what I want, it boots not to complain. |

step into : <u>sprays</u> (boughs) that <u>look</u> too

<u>lofty</u> : <u>suck</u> the soil's fertility : <u>wholesome</u>

flowers : <u>is fore-run with</u> : <u>a pale</u>, <u>in compass</u>
            ₂    ₁

<u>of</u> (a paling) : <u>choked up</u> : <u>unpruned</u> :

<u>knots</u> (flower knots)  he hath <u>met with</u> (it has   5

come upon him) : sound these news (tell these news) :

to divine (guess) : <u>post</u> you <u>to</u> London [post <u>to</u> .. <u>on</u>]

<u>unsay</u> : if that thy valour <u>stand on</u> <u>sympathies</u> :

to <u>turn to</u>, <u>turn on</u>, [<u>turn</u> thy ♪ <u>on</u> me] : <u>brandish</u> :

mine honour's <u>pawn</u> (token) : to <u>tie</u> thee <u>to</u> : grant  10

their <u>suit</u> : <u>figure of</u> (substitute for) : a

<u>surety for</u> : to <u>tutor to</u> this submission : I

have <u>worn</u> so many winters <u>out</u> : a <u>brittle</u>

glory :

     <u>Is II</u>. ⓔⓟ<u>exalted</u> [sweetˢ: love beauty]  15
         innocence
<u>forsaken</u> [sweetˢ] : <u>house of</u> (abode of) : <u>plenteous</u>
             [maiden]
[ ♪ , beauty fondness tenderˢ] : <u>soothsayer</u> ˏ <u>full</u>

<u>of</u> [love truth] : <u>endless</u> [grace] : <u>fenced</u> : so

<u>utterly</u> [sweet] : the <u>captain of fifty</u> : I will

give .. to be : [ 🖊 eyes so] <u>cunningly</u> [<u>contrived</u> that.] :

<u>provoking</u> [fairness] : [her] <u>show</u> (mien) : <u>oppressive</u> [eyes]

ruling [beauty] : to <u>beat to pieces</u> : <u>pleading</u> :

<u>excellently</u> : <u>choicest</u> : <u>pleasant plant</u> : [my dear]

<u>captivitity</u> : <u>measureless</u> [shot of joy] : <u>speeding</u>　　　　5

[blood]: drawing [glance] : waste place [to seem a] :
　　　　　　　　strong cords
　　[glances [irresistible chains of light wh drew

me close] : <u>blossom</u> : undone [<u>undoing</u> 🎵 ] :

<u>purged</u> : <u>wasting</u> [ 🎵 ] : <u>wasting, wearing</u> [fondˢ]


Sh. Rd II.　my wife to France from whence <u>set forth</u>　　10

in pomp, she came : and <u>piece</u> the way <u>out with</u>

a heavy heart : <u>Kill</u> thy heart :


　Sc. Kenil　　<u>conjure away</u> — <u>lay them</u> — <u>swathed</u>

<u>with</u> a <u>hay wisp</u> : <u>whimpering</u> : <u>defoul</u> :

<u>parry</u> advice : <u>taking the wall</u> of a woman　　　　15

(slighting her) : <u>the full blow</u> of her dignity
a champion to the very
　ᴧoutrance : spell over thy splendour :

court or congregation : probing : feast :

pay : alchemy : this light o' love :

had <u>hurt his interest</u> with her :

    Sc. L of I.  a <u>milder</u> pang : to <u>chafe</u>

<u>thee</u> : in minstrel <u>line</u> :                                             5


<u>Jer</u>: II ⓓ <u>Cry in</u> the ears of : they are

<u>gone far from</u> me, & have <u>walked after</u>

vanity : [the love, grief] <u>found in</u> me : they

that <u>handle</u> the law : walk<sup>go</sup> after things that

<u>do not profit</u> : <u>plead with</u> : thine iniq. is <u>marked</u>     10

<u>before</u> me : <u>gaddest</u> thou : III,  In the ways

hast thou <u>sat for</u> them : IV <u>put away</u> : <u>turned</u>

<u>unto</u> me : to <u>fall upon</u> you : shall <u>walk with</u>

the house of Israel : <u>put thee among</u> : publish

<u>against</u> : <u>give out against</u> :                                 15


    <u>Barnes</u>.  rim : <u>shrinken</u> moss : the

<u>leanen</u> apple tree : his <u>bow'd</u> tail : sprack :

her shade a-whiv'ren black : overright :

avore : slooe : back in May :


Jer V & VI. ⓓ  Are not thine eyes upon the truth?

[fixed my ♪ upon thee, hope &c] : to the full : [so]

given to [sweetness as she] : to try [one] :                5

        Dic: brought me down : brought out

tears : bring upon : to bring to : to get the

better of : to beat up (for recruits) : to beat about

(wander) : to be out (mistaken) : all along :

they are at me : [to at any one] ♭                10

        Sc: show (sight) : to wind through : o'er

his features glance convulsions : bore away

(went away) : a silence dead sunk on the wood :

drew to, (went to) : the winter worn o'er [to wear

through the w.] : to sway (mind of) :                15


  Barnes. the græglc's bell : sky-blue :

to fay wrong : underneath the showers : drong :

whivered : my memory shall make 'em good :

a staddle : avore : cwoffer : the reaves

(of a waggon) : athirt : settle : fusty : a tutty :

kitty-boots : spry : a tait :


Ier:⁽ˡⁱᵈ⁾ to your hurt : to set one's [heart, name,]          5

lift up a cry : make cakes to the queen of h.

[give hours to thee] : see what I did to it :

to be well with : take up a lamentation :

came into my heart : to fray away : to

spread before (show) : slidden back : given to :          10

to put to silence [into gloom] : is not her king

in her (Zion)? : the hurt : astonishᵗ hath

taken hold on me : a lodging place : wayfaring

to know thy mind : to do for : [gloomy years lie

in wait for ...] : visit upon : to cut off [𝄐 &c] :          15

to fall upon (attack) : glory in [her 𝄐 gloried in its

perfect home] : let him that glorieth glory in this :

to delight in : ⓘⓧ

<u>Dic</u>:  to <u>call for</u> (request) : to <u>call in</u> : to <u>call up</u>

(past days) : <u>call off</u> (thoughts from) : to <u>call together</u>

(the diffᵗ happy hours ..) : to <u>care for</u> : to <u>carry high</u> :

<u>carry</u> me <u>away</u> : <u>carry back</u> to : <u>carry</u> me <u>down</u>

<u>to</u> future years : <u>carry forth</u> : [her eyes <u>carried f.</u> the    5

tale of her heart] : to <u>carry on</u> : days may <u>carry</u>

<u>out</u> the dream : <u>cast aside, away</u> : <u>cast off</u> old ways :

<u>cast down</u> : to <u>cast up</u> (probabilities, likelihoods of) :

<u>caught at</u>  𝄐 as at something ... to <u>clear from</u> : to <u>clear</u>

my brow <u>for</u> thee : to <u>close with</u> (heart closed w. h) :    10

to <u>countenance</u> : to <u>course</u> : to <u>creep out</u> : to <u>cry</u>

<u>down</u> : to <u>cry up</u> : ☺


   <u>F. Q.</u>  <u>it fortuned</u> : to <u>weld</u> or <u>wield</u> : cries

he <u>threw forth</u> : to <u>play about</u> :

<u>Sha</u> [dew drops <u>stand on</u> many a leaf & droop from    15

many a blade] to <u>use</u> sins : every tongue <u>brings</u>

<u>in</u> a <u>several</u> tale : has twice <u>done</u> salutation :

dreams .. <u>entered in</u> : the foe <u>vaunts</u> in the field :

to <u>cope with</u> [love coped with reason &c] <u>amaze</u>

the welkin :

<u>Buch</u>:  to <u>think out</u> (a puzzle) :

stale (maid)   to fleet :      <u>By</u>:  to see into :

<u>Dic</u>.  to <u>do away with</u> : <u>do up</u> :      5

have <u>to do with</u> : <u>do without</u> : to <u>drag in</u>

(name, life) : <u>draw aside</u> : <u>draw down</u> ( ♪ ) :

to <u>draw up</u> ( ♪ schemes) : to <u>feel for</u> :

to <u>fetch up</u> (thoughts) : to <u>fit out</u> : to <u>fit with</u> :

to <u>get abroad</u> (known) : <u>get clear</u> : <u>get up</u> :      10

to <u>give ground</u> : to <u>give oneself to</u> : to <u>give</u>

<u>place</u> : <u>give over</u> : to <u>give forth</u> : <u>give out</u> :

<u>given up to</u> : <u>went abroad</u> : <u>went beyond</u>

(my hope) : to <u>go off</u> = <u>fall off</u> : <u>go through</u>

(endure) : Ⓖ      15

<u>Is</u>.(ᵉᵖ)<u>confederate</u> charms : <u>taken against</u> me :

my <u>uttermost</u> hour, even to his <u>uttermost</u> hope :

<u>desolate</u> days, <u>desolate</u> eyes (of happˢ), <u>desolate</u>

body (of charms by age) : <u>nourishing</u> eyes, glance

sweetness :

abundant hours of ♪ , glances of ♪ , beauty :

the abundant blushes : loving-place : briars :

the mattock : if years be faithful unto me,

... but if they fail .. : the familiar thought :
                              moving
a peeping hope : cheeks of living red : ⑧                    5

   [blushes wandered to my heart & back again]

[it cannot stand (endure] took to me.

   Is:⁽ᵉᵖ⁾ the nations = the globe, the world.

shiny : you multiply my tears : to joy : the

yoke of ⎰loneliness : stoutness : destroying years :      10
          ⎱fondness
lifting joy : needy heart : robbing time : those

·  excelling times : 'the glory of his high looks.'

   ♪ put down by time : 'a valiant man' : leanness
'kindle
   ₐa burning" : 'his fruitful field' : a standard bearer'

few, that a child may write [tell] them : an over-         15

flowing heart: our determined ♪ : yoking ♪ :
              wish
the anointing softness of thy words : shake his hand

against : laid up thought : lopped my hope⊗:

such determined sweetness, flowing sweetness :

as my mind <u>makes towards</u> thee, — as I

<u>make towards</u> age :

   <u>Is</u>:<sup>(ep)</sup>woe unto kisses : to turn aside

a tear, fondness, thought of me : needy

heart, her needy eyes, glance, my needy       5

lips, her needy beauty : my hope died

childless : I left my hope on .. : bowed

down by 🎵 : if I fall under : 🎵 is a

moaning thing : a kingly thought : the

fruit of (result of) : stout resolve : high       10

fondness : prudent brained fondness : that

excellent treasurer, my heart : hewers down
    strong
of first resolve (her eyes) : death the hewer —

time, a child with a new axe, who hews

the sweetest : those briery thoughts, (reason,)      15
    hurt
that tear my hope : my thin remnant when

hope & beauty gone : smiting : virtues,

"the outcasts : eyes so mighty in speech : ⓧⓘ

Lucr:  the gliding constellations : unveil

the day, open the day, uncover the day :

spring into sight, life : fling upon, fling at :

crisis of eyes & heat : this system of pain :

　　ɪ Sam. 26.  to tell on, upon : said　　　　　5

in my heart :

　　Swin:  the thing beforetime seen : from

the midmost of Ida : I shall never be

friends again with roses. (beauty here from

contrast of colloq! phrase with high thought)　　10

```
fair \     / deep
       X
face /     \ thought
```

overblown : bared thy beauties to : fain (high)

　　A pres. introd by 'where' —
　　　　　　As the lost white feverish limbs ⚹　　15
　　　　　　Of the Lesbian Sappho, adrift
　　　　　　In foam where the seaweed swims ⚹
　　　　　　Swam loose for the streams to lift

　　You kill men's hearts : carve (make) :

whet : dumb under axe or dart : on this　　　　20

wise : gone thorough (through) : a privy way :

eyelids
‸shot through with purple (marked th.) comelier :

feet pashed the mire : earth clear of years that

 wrong her : fates (woes) : [instant = trice

 pulse, beat,] lids = eyelids : the stooped urn,

 (dipping) sad blosoms : the slow blood :    5

 'the slow delicious bright soft blood' : 'bathing
   1  2   3  4

 the spices' : 'drink till the lapping leaves are

 reddened" : the date of us (length of lives) :

 trapped : iron sides falter (decay) : periods

 (ages) : latter men : lift up thy lips (contrast  10

of great action with little object. e.g. raise

up thy lids, pull in a kiss from me 𝄢 , a

tear moved off its eye :

  'Of all things tired thy lips look weariest

  Save the long smile that they are wearied of.'  15

  A pleasure house (the body) : in what

swift wise (in what a swift way) : sometime

(at sometime or other) : 'I know not how this

last month leaves your hair', as the hour

left me, the day bade sad farewell : "love <u>kissed</u>

<u>out</u> by pleasure", I wept out seasons : that has
                                             no heart :
    <u>Ezek</u>: 27.  the event came to me :

    Ezek I.  I was among the tearful :

  ſ <u>was among</u> my dreams : <u>the hand of</u> ſ       5

<u>was on</u> me : <u>the hand of</u> thought <u>was on</u> me :

a delight <u>was about</u> it : went up and down

among : 'twas as it were : so sweet that it

was mournful : when I was <u>full of</u> sighs for :

wherever I go, the pain <u>goes by</u> me : went : stood    10

it had brightness, pain, <u>in it</u> : doubts <u>are with</u>

me : I <u>sent a</u> thought <u>to</u> her, him, glance <u>to</u> h. :

'I have <u>made</u> thy face <u>strong against</u> their f.'

he <u>made</u> the time <u>strong against</u> me, put

thy ℓ strong against my ℓ / I wᵈ not <u>receive</u>    15

the doubt, thought : '<u>strong upon</u> me' : it <u>came</u>

<u>to me</u> like a .,, (the thought c.) : ſ made me a

watcher, ſ {made me his watchman weary :
              {chose me

hope made me a watchman unto ſ that night : I shall

require ✒ at his eyes : to turn from ✒  might

went out of me : my heart w. o. o. m.   my life

w. o. o. m. & followed him : my old hopes will

be to me a scourge : I laid my ⎰ age  ⎱ life before ⎰ time

me, (think of ..)  cast scorn against me : to          5

set against : to lay upon one (impress upon) :

to lay out to (to tell) : drove my light away :

consume away : you will be against me : thou

wilt go out of me (shall forget) : the last

⎰ hue of thee went out of ~~my~~ me then : I          10
⎱remnant

rest upon you : unsparing eyes : the last part

of thy soul will go out of my soul : when thy

soul came into mine : when thine eyes,/ speech/

words/ accomplished their work in me ☌: lay

waste my years, charms, beauty, days : an          15

astonishment to them : send upon me the ... :

a flit of mirth passed through me :

VI.

Swin: "leave thee = make thee (memorable)

sisters .. grave as pasturing fawns that

feed & fear some arrow : at whiles (at times)

she .. cheeks & lips & eyelids kisses her :

savours (smells) : lands loved of summer :

unfooted ways : at one with : thankworthy :                   5

unleashed : seen <u>otherwhere</u> : wild heights

untravelled of the wind; & vales cloven seaward

by their violent streams : for silver nor

bright snow nor feather of foam was whiter,

(for neither silver &c) : an evil blossom :                  10

     For an evil blossom was born

     Of sea foam & the frothing of blood,

     Blood-red & bitter of fruit,

     And the seed of it laughter & tears,

     And the leaves of it madness & scorn;            15

     A bitter flower from the bud

       Sprung of the sea without root,

       Sprung without graft from the years.

         (Love)

thunder of storm" : [the sweet of lips] : wailing

of wives : clamour of currents : eyeshot :

the first of the morning ($1^{st}$ goer out in morn$^g$) :

rise, rest, and are & are not : Would God :

nor the spoil of slain things, nor the fame :                5

who gives a star & takes a sun away : Meleager

like a sun in spring that strikes branch into leaf

[drives out the buds, draws forth the leaves] : the

green ooze of a sun-struck marsh shook with

a thousand reeds untunable : up in heaven : much        10

desire divided him (made him feeble in his shot) :

bride-bound to the gods (wedded into the fam. of gods)

they saw no trail nor scented [Admis.] : the

sudden string (sud$^y$ loosed s.)  the waterish air

(damp) [watery] : tense : the roar of wintering          15

streams [like a winter-bourne] (The plu. often

makes a common word novel as grasses, dews,)

blossoms cleaving to the sod : [to brush e.g. brush

my ↶ with ⌀ ⌒⌄ : hours that marry dawn

& noon : [braids (hair)] : [to fall off (fade)] : shall

I put back my day? : out weep heaven at

rainiest : kinship :

> Part of Chorus.

But up in heaven the high gods one by one          5

Lay hands upon the draught that quickeneth,

> Fulfilled with all tears shed and all things done,

>> And stir with soft imperishable breath

>> The bubbling bitterness of life and death,

And hold it to our lips and laugh; but they          10

Preserve their lips from tasting night or day

> Lest they too change & sleep, the fates that spun,

The lips that made us and the hands that slay;

>> Lest all these change, & heaven bow down to none,

Change & be subject to the secular sway          15

>> And terrene revolution of the sun.

> Therefore they thrust it from them, putting time away.


I would the wine of time, made sharp & sweet

With multitudinous days & nights & tears

    And many mixing savours of strange years,

Were no more trodden of them under feet,

      Cast out & spilt about their holy places:

That life were given them as a fruit to eat        5

    And death to drink as water; that the light

    Might ebb, drawn backward from their eyes, & night

      Hide for one hour the imperishable faces.

    That they might rise up sad in heaven, & know

    Sorrow & sleep, one paler than young snow,    10

      One cold as blight of dew & ruinous rain;

Rise up & rest & suffer a little, and be

Awhile as all things born with us and we

    And grieve as men, & like slain men be slain.


For now we know not of them; but one saith    15

    The gods are gracious, praising God; and one

When hast thou seen? or hast thou felt his breath

    Touch, nor consume thine eyelids as the sun

Nor fill thee to the lips with fiery death?

    None hath beheld him, none

Seen above other gods and shapes of things,

Swift without feet & flying without wings,

Intolerable, not clad with death or life,         5

    Insatiable, not known of night or day,

The lord of love & loathing & of strife

    Who gives a star & takes a sun away;

Who shapes the soul, & makes her a barren wife

    To the earthly body & grievous growth of clay;    10

Who turns the large limbs to a little flame

    And binds the great sea with a little sand;

Who makes desire, and slays desire with shame;

    Who shakes the heaven as ashes in his hand;

Who seeing the light & shadow for the same,    15

    Bids day waste night as fire devours a brand

Smites without sword, & scourges without rod;

        The supreme evil, God.

<u>Sc</u>. amid the pealing <u>conquest-cry</u>.  to meaner

<u>front</u> was ne'er assigned such mastery o'er

the common mind : whence that light? (came t. l.)

the sound <u>swings</u> over land & sea : a glade whose

<u>tangled alleys</u> : <u>faintly</u> blue [freshly white,                5

( ⌒ ) redly soft, wisely grey ( ∠ )]


<u>Swin</u>. <u>Chast</u>:  I think of that as dead men

of good days  Ere <u>the wrong side of death</u>

<u>was theirs</u>, when God Was friends with them :

<u>point lips</u> at him :                                              10

Queen. — No words? no pity—

Have you no mercies for such men? God help!

It seems I am the meekest heart on earth—

Yea, the one tender woman left alive,

And knew it not. I will not let him live,                        15

For all my pity of him.

[Finding that what we condemned as little in us,

is in truth greater than others'], that what we

blamed is not blameable but great: e.g. going to the

P. Meeting that even$^g$ & not finding the Perkins's there

having been blaming self for wish to stay away, also

cutting Arch$^{\underline{e}}$ if successf:]

                              Now three years since      5

[executing]

This͜had not seemed so good an end for me;

But in some wise all things wear round betimes

And wind up well : ~~her n~~.

             Her name that turns my face

to fire, being written : I know <u>no whit</u> how      10

 much : to <u>gird at</u> : meseems : face drawn

up about the eyes as if they sucked the cheeks :

flowertime : the supple <u>way</u> she hath [the

blushing, blue-eyed way she has] : sky colour

a saint<u>ship</u> (a saint) : laced : some slow      15

heavy kiss that plucks the heart out at the lips :

sweeter than <u>all sorts of life</u> : love was <u>fellow</u>

<u>with</u> my flesh.

        enbloom.

[Sweetly say us the rote of love.]

(adjs)
&
<u>Thes</u>. (subs.) soft <u>accent</u> of thy heart : sweet

<u>ache</u> of n—k, l–p, s—l : soft <u>acts</u> : swift

acts of thy 🖎 : warm } <u>action</u> of pulse, blush :
⎧ swift ⎫
⎩ rapid ⎭

acute §§§§§ sweet, blood, blush : the <u>add</u>                    5

of red : the <u>added</u> sweet : adding Kisses :

the hot <u>ado</u> of blushes : the sharp <u>ado</u> of

sweet & bitter : the dear adulteries of lid

with lid, pleasure & regret, white & red

(on cheek) : <u>afflux</u> of heart to heart : <u>agile</u>        10

laughter, <u>agile</u> meanings from eyes : <u>agile</u>

eyes, pants, years, hours : sweet <u>agonies</u> : thy

fresh air : <u>airy</u> laugh, touch : <u>alert</u> flush

<u>ample</u> arms : <u>arc</u> of brow : sobbing } striving

<u>artery</u> : quick <u>ascent</u> of blood : beats of       15

soul : beating kisses : <u>beck</u> of eye :

<u>bend</u> of mouth, sweet <u>bends</u> of neck :

<u>besetting wants</u> of thee, bes 𝆑 eyes :
for

braced together⎱
few <u>bits</u> of cheek : <u>bind</u> of hair : the <u>brace</u>⎰

between us : <u>breaks</u> of breath : breaths of

kiss : brim of thy mouth : the <u>cadence</u>

of thy life in thee : <u>calms</u> between rushing

kisses : a <u>calm</u> kiss : <u>capering</u> thrills                    5

stings⎱ within : <u>capers</u> of blood : the
bites ⎰
<u>biting</u> want : <u>catch</u> of lip by lip : long

kisses & short <u>ceasings</u> : sweet <u>chafe</u>

of .. : <u>chills</u> : close <u>circuits</u> of me :

a <u>clap</u> of pain : <u>clear</u> eyes : the long           10

<u>cleaving</u>, eager <u>cleavings</u> together : the close
                              thine
of arms abᵗ me : soft closes of∧eye :

slow closes of thy lips on ... ; long low

<u>close</u> of a k—— : k——s with their long

low <u>closes</u> : <u>coil</u> of arms abᵗ me : growth          15

of <u>colour</u> from the clasp : the <u>come & go</u> of ...

coo<u>l</u> tears, lips, breaths : <u>course</u> over

<u>course</u> of k—— : long <u>courses</u> of k——

crowing for ☝ : fair <u>curves</u>, white <u>curves</u> :

sweet <u>cut</u> of pain : lip ⎫ dally with ⎰lip
                 mouth⎭         ⎱mouth

long <u>dance of</u> sweets, pulse : <u>deep</u> eyes : <u>deep</u>

<u>thirst</u> for ... : deep <u>dells</u> of thy hair, : <u>dense</u>

delight : fair <u>devices</u> on thy face : <u>dim</u>

↗ , <u>dim</u> kiss : <u>dip</u> of thy lip into mine : deep      5

dips : <u>dip</u> into thy neck : soft <u>dip</u> of thy
⎰neck
⎱throat : as thy bosom dipped & filled : dip
    ⎰dry of k——s :
me ⎱away in k——s : <u>draw</u> ↶ over ↶ :

<u>drifts</u> of hair : long <u>drinks</u> of : dumb

⌒ for weariness : moving <u>dyes</u> :      10

blood <u>eddys</u> about me : roses have <u>eked</u>

out to lilies : <u>elect</u> sweets : <u>empty</u> soul :

soft <u>ends</u> of thy hair : <u>enter</u> on ↗ : escapes

of breath : <u>even</u> brow : this dear <u>evil</u>, this

↗ :ⓔ      15

    <u>Rickm:</u>  the <u>set</u> of thy head : <u>fine</u>-drawn

kisses : sweep of lip : soft suck of thy mouth

(lip) on mine, suck k——s from my mouth :

sweet <u>bell</u> inside that told of waiting feasts :

flowered braids : curly lengths of hair : eyes ⟩ᵏ⁻ˢ

of richest execution : worked pale by k— :

carved work, vein-work in thy neck : fragile

sobs : fragile nos : profuse swee— : canopies

of thy eyes : drip of tears : coming & returning          5

of breast : the finish of thy face :

      Thes & Sw

  [the day found me— : the day sought to ... the

day forgot, remembered : the day loved .. : the days

stood : the day bade, the day watched : the years          10

ranked up themselves] Sw: the dewfall : lightened

with laughter : "And May with her world in

flower" : [and May had made ready : the roses

all fever sick (w. heat) & the trees all weary of
    the month of ~~the~~
toying]ₐthe long decline of roses : [your face          15

the colour of years-old hope :

    The head of a smile.

    Swin (M̶)

kissed out : August blue : green miles.

<u>Swin.</u>

<u>pricked</u> at lip with tender red : <u>jets</u> =

rises up : <u>deep</u> scent :

Triumph of Time —

. . . . . .

O brother the gods were good to you                    5

   Sleep & be glad while the world endures

Be well content as the years wear through;

   Give thanks for life & the loves & lures;

Give thanks for life O brother & death

   For the sweet last sound of her feet, her breath    10

For gifts she gives you gracious & few,

   Tears & kisses that lady of yours.

Rest, & be glad of the gods; but I

   How shall I praise them or how take rest?

There is not room under all the sky                    15

   For me that know not of worst or best,

Dream or desire of the days before

Sweet things or bitterness any more.

Love will not come to me now though I die,

    As love comes close to you breast to breast

    —  —  —  —  —  —  —

I shall go my ways—tread out my measure,

    Fill the days of my daily breath           5

With fugitive things not good to treasure

    Do as the world doth, say as it saith;

But if we had loved each other—O sweet

Had you felt lying under the palms of your feet,

The heart of my heart, beating harder with pleasure    10

    To feel you tread it to dust & death—

Ah, had I not taken my life up & given

    All that life gives & the years let go

The wine & honey—the balm & leaven

    The dreams reared high & the hopes brought low?   15

Come life, come death, not a word be said;

    Should I lose you living & vex you dead?

I never shall tell you on earth; & in heaven

If I cry to you then will you hear or know?

¶ A mirth. <u>Sha</u>.

<u>Swin</u>: <u>beyond</u> (in time) : years fell <u>past</u> :

fair cheeks, & leaves them <u>grey</u>.                              5

<u>lithe</u> : <u>pores</u> : <u>dew</u> of lip.

<u>Thes</u>. <u>fabulously</u> sweet : delicate <u>fabric</u>

of thine eye, skin, cheek : thy ⎰sweet
⎱cheek's

<u>facility</u> ⎰in reds & whites : <u>facile</u>
⎱of

blushes : a worthy <u>facing</u> for me : rare          10

fair
<u>factory</u> of soft words. :ᴧ<u>factory</u> of tears :

<u>faithless</u> red : <u>faithless</u> beauty : <u>fall</u>

of hair, <u>fall</u> of eye, hue : <u>fall</u> of foot :

<u>fall</u> of lid on lid, lash on lash : <u>fall</u> of

tears : words of that sweet <u>family</u> :                      15

whole <u>family</u> of sobs : delicate sobs :

<u>famine</u> of fulfilments, flush of wishes :

familiar as mouth with ^smiles^ : fan of

thy fresh breathings : (far)

Carl. Dan: the fear wh issued from

her look : between Feltro & Feltro

(Montefeltro) : quits the thing commenced :                    5

with thinking I wasted the enterprise :

so fair & blessed that I prayed her to

command : single in worth : flowerets

when the sun whitens them :

   Barnes.  the wild daisies a-spread in a                   10

sheet [the wide sheet of stars, sheets of moonlight]

the brook that did slide [sliding stars, blushes,

beauties, hopes] : blocks o' rock : a love-child :

noontide's glare [the glare of the day] work I had

on hand [love, sorrow I have on (in) hand] : the       15

vootless groves [the footed street] : that her

face may put a former year in place [put in

place my hope again] : to sink upon (fall upon) :

when the hours o' night wer vew [the

even.s nearly touched the morns] : a milker :

stars a winken, day a <u>shrinken</u> [my 🎵
       less
for thee shrinks<sub>∧</sub>every day] : [night <u>kept away</u>

the landscape from my eyes] : clouds a-comen     5

up [wind coming up, blushes, thoughts] :

<u>for</u> = (in place of) woone a comen up <u>for</u>

woone a gone : [[blown out thistles]]

[forlorn as a blown-out dandelion]

                    I was
   <u>Ps</u>. 4. et seq. 'set me <u>at liberty</u> when<sub>∧</sub>in    10

trouble' [tears, set free from grief, sorrow]

sorrow has <u>chosen me</u> to itself : talk to

mine own heart, commune with my displeasure:

beseeched her displeasure to —— : '<u>put</u> gladness
              {years upon her
<u>in</u> my heart : it <u>put</u> {blushes on her cheek,    15

you <u>put</u> white where red was : my calling

(my voice) : I <u>have no pleasure in</u> eyes, lips :
     {time
lead {sorrow <u>away from</u> her, <u>lead</u> me <u>to</u> sorʷ:

abear |: thy <u>favourable</u> kindness, <u>favourable</u>

ablaze| : eyes, shape, days : her hope, love,

abler     <u>looked up</u> again : <u>work</u> love :

<u>save</u> her <u>from</u> time : time, the world, hap.

<u>deal friendly</u> with her : love was sore       5

<u>put to</u> then : I have <u>put by</u> faith : like
            crumble
{dreams that {die in handling : like tunes
{hoar         {waste   being thought of
            fade
in the mind that die being tried


<u>Sha</u>   tart : to cap : [the dinted moon] to hack :

timelier [timeliest] : I have ever held       10

my cap off to thy fortunes ⁊ : to lip :


<u>Sha:</u>   What majesty is in her gait? Remember

   If e'er thou look'dst on majesty, ⁊ :

     Did it from his teeth, ⁊ :


scantly : a breather : nuncio.        15

To <u>cool</u> a gipsy's lust, ⁊

[(sun) to darken leaves — fade flowers :

to kiss him out of love—& k, & k, & k.

him out of love : will hasten ~~to thee~~

to make sweet futures mournful pasts :                5

I would sweet havings brought not bitter

hads : to wear out love by loving : gone

to tire her eyes with him :]

<u>Sha</u>: For want of <u>other</u> idleness ⁊

S.R  "They are <u>at one</u> (opposed to at issue)        10

C. Reade.  'The wrinkled sea.'

<u>Concoc</u>: from Hab.ᵏ violent kisses : delight

too <u>violent</u> for me : violent days : she <u>showed</u>

<u>me</u> smiles : I thought what the <u>turned</u> years

had <u>showed</u> me: her red spoilt eyes : her         15

lips slack with sorrow : if time would slack

a little : his love is slacked : the fall of mouth

upon mouth : the fall of time : there never go

forth from you pleasant {tears {speeches : whatever the

years may tell : the end of her pulses : the end of          5

her eyes : your heart will rock, sway, wave on in

its {same {low sweet pace is mine wild heavy or still

Is it I to chide you that these things show? Is it

I to chide that you took me {ill {so, wear me down?

that you are among the light, meek : work sweet          10

work : lips my lips' dwelling place : you raised

up heats in me — hopes of haste : "ye will not be-

lieve though it be told you" : hasty pants : hasty

treads : hasty heart : marches of pleasure, march

into death, the grave : march through the years,          15

march through your beauty : the ~~breadth~~ length of your

beauty, how many {days, the ~~length~~ breadth how many {minds

{minds : how many years does your beauty {possess? {days            do            beauties {own

how many hopes not theirs?   I. 5.

C. Pr̠ᵣ. concoc: fair <u>offenders</u> : soberly

("said he', soberly") : err : 'a mighty salvation'

forefathers : 'day spring' : endue : concord :

assaults : adversaries : chosen, chosen

mate, chosen {man / lad : governance : a       5

<u>lowly</u> young lad like him : '<u>turned</u> the

captivity of Zion', <u>turned</u> the gloom : /

'<u>maketh much of</u>' : <u>hindrance</u> of his {mind / life :

'money upon usury' : shall never <u>fall</u> : all

his <u>delight was in</u> : <u>run after</u> fashion, love :       10

<u>inheritance</u> : lot that <u>fell to</u> : 'night season',

night time, day time, spring season, summer s :

a feigned future, a feigned past, a feigned

expectance : 'the path of life' :   Ps. 15. 16.

'Our separation so abides & flies       15

That thou residing here go'st yet with me

And I, hence fleeting, here remain with thee.'

                              A & C.

'My becomings kill me, when they do not

Eye well to you'              A & C.


'All of a man that regrets, & all of a maid that allures'.

                                        Swin.

'Those eyes, the greenest of things blue              5

     The bluest of things grey'.

                                        Swin.

Before thee the laughter, behind thee the

tears of desire  (To Love)              Swin


'To the deeds in his soul as the ripening sun'.       10

                                        Isa C.

'His imperfection his defence'

                                        Sc.

You had rather lose your wits to do me harm

Than keep sound wits to help me              15

                                        Swin.

'The pleasure that some fathers feed upon

Is my strict fast'              Sha

'We three are but thyself'      Sha

'To see her is to love her'     Bu.                    5

'Thought is speech, & speech is truth.' Sc.


'To fear the foe, since fear oppress$^{\text{th}}$ strength

Gives in your weakness, strength unto yʳ foe'.

                                        Sh.

'Who makes desire, & slays desire with shame'

                                        Swin.        10

'Fear & be slain: no worse can come to fight.

And fight & die, is death destroying death'.

                                        Sh.

Silvius— Sweet Phœbe, pity me.

Phebe. Why I am sorry for thee, gentle Silvius.

Sil. Wherever sorrow is, relief $\begin{cases}\text{[might]}\\ \text{would}\end{cases}$ be;

    If you do sorrow at my grief in love,

        By giving love, your sorrow and my grief

        Were both extermined.     A.Y.L.I. Sha.

5

           Faster than his tongue

    Did make offence, his eye did heal it up

           A.Y.L.I. Sha.

    Who tells me true, though in his tale lie death

    I hear him as he flattered [speaking false]

10

           A & C.

.. The present pleasure

By revolution lowering, does become

The opposite of itself: she's good, being gone.

15

           A & C.

    The hated, grown to strength

Are newly grown to love.     A & C.

        My becoming

Hangs weights upon my tongue.   Sha.

Cupid have mercy                    Sha

Say March may wed September

  And Time divorce regret       Swin.

                    I will kiss thy lips;                    5

Haply, some poison yet doth hang on them

  To make me die with a restorative

                    Sha.

              Something it is I would—

O, my oblivion is a very Anthony,                    10

And I am all forgotten

                    A & C.    Sha

Some tear or laugh ere lip & eye were man's

                    Swin.

          [beauties]
Oh, all these,ₐand all the body, and all the soul to that

                    Swin                    16

Merch$^t$ of Venice.

<u>Ant</u>.  I hold the world but as the world Gratiano;

A stage, where every man must play a part,

And mine a sad one.

> (obs. the natural drawing-in of thought)     5
> from world to self)

<u>Por</u>.  Good sentences & well pronounced

<u>Ner</u>.  They w$^d$ be better if well followed

also

Lady to D$^r$ Johnson who asked her if she was

going to write another work beside the one she showed him—

"I have other irons in fire".     11

                /other irons."
D$^r$ J. "I w$^d$ recommend you to put this with your

In both the repartee depends upon a

minute & literal regard of the preceding words,
    remotely
added$_\wedge$to the speaker's immediate object.     15

Portia concerning her suitors— There is not

one among them but I dote on his very

absence.

Wear prayer books in my pocket —

[talk {in psalm lines : think of Sunday
    {~~psalm tunes~~

afternoons when they dwell on merry times :

hum psalm tunes when they are overtaken

                    least bawdy

in liquor. (reverse):— pick out the ∧song       5

he knows—one with no b. words, only

         "I

suggestions : never ~~goes~~ further than a

plain damn on Sundays—no, you've

never heard me do more than that" :

Walk going-to-church pace : eats all his    10

meals as sacraments in Church :

think of hymns when people say 'a

pleasant song'.]    sighs hymn tunes with

a drawn lip.

"If your love do not persuade you to come    15

let not my letter." (letʳ of Antonio to Bassanio.)

: thy currish spirit <u>governed</u> a wolf :

<u>Much Ado &c.</u>     <u>Don John.</u> " ... Though I

cannot be said to be a flattering honest man

it must not be denied but I am a plain dealing

villain" [though you may deny me the name

of {a flattering lover

{loving, you must own that I have shown          5

some tenderness in my hate]


L. L. L.

"She must <u>lie</u> here" (abide)

  ['We be lyen at the Chequers' Hʸ Hand]

    'Tis long of you that. ['Tis all along of you that'     10
                                                  Colloq.]
    "A snip" = a bit


The four complexions in this play (223).

⸘ such, as the classes of loveables —

naming a number as if it had always

been definitely laid down (by a lady          15

novelist pps.)

A charʳ with something of Costard's

conceit & modesty & love of right understᵍ·

(Edwᵈ Cox, pps)  i.e.: —

"Cost.  I Pompey am, Pompey surnamed the big

Dumain.  The great                                    5
   [nodding placidly]
Cost ˄ It is great, Sir;— Pompey surnamed &c

      x    x    x    x    x

Princess.  Great thanks, great Pompey.

Cos.  'Tis not so much worth; but I hope

   I was perfect: I made a little fault in

   great."          (305)                           10


     Dull's character:—

"Dull.  Which is the duke's own person?

Biron.  This fellow; What woulds't?

Dull.  I myself reprehend his own person,

   for I am his grace's tharborough: but I          15

   wᵈ see his own person in flesh & blood."

               (216)

Moth's charʳ:—

"<u>Armado</u>. Boy what sign is it when a man of

great spirit grows melanchʸ?

<u>Moth</u>. A great sign, Sir, that he will look sad.

<u>Arm</u>. Why sadness is one & the selfsame thing, dear imp.

<u>Moth</u>. No, no; O lord! Sir, no."          (220)          6


Armado's charʳ

<u>Arm</u> Is there not a ballad, boy, of the King

& the Beggar? ..... I will have

that subject newly writ o'er that I

may example my digression by some          10

mighty precedent. Boy, I do love

that country girl. ...          (224)


Holofernes charʳ

<u>Nathaniel</u>. A rare talent! ....

<u>Holo</u>. This is a gift that I have, simple          15

simple; a foolish extravagant spirit,

full of forms, figures, shapes, objects,

ideas, apprehensions, motions, revolutions

...... But the gift is good in those

in whom it is acute, & I am thankful

for it."                    (256)                         5

Biron, at the thought of his oath, when

he sees his fellows in love too:—

"God amend us, God amend! we

are much out of the way."        (263)

Walpole's Letters & Reminiscences.        10

(Sept 68)

1. Schulemberg ⟶✗⟵ Geo I  ⟶✗⟶ Sophia Dorothea
   Duch of Kendal  /  1714   ( ✗ Count Konigsmark;
2. Kilmansegge ✗                    murdered)
   C. of Darlington                                    15
1. Mrs Howard during Q's life ⟶✗⟶ Geo II ⟶✗⟶ Caroline
2. Walmoden, C. of Yarmouth ⟶✗          died 1737
   after Q's death

77

clanging thunder, humble bee : pealing waves

whooping storm : clicking twigs ; flapping

of leaves ; creaking of trunks, & wrenching
                                                wind
of branches : booming wind : hum of rain                    5

undertones of wind : hoarse & husky storm :

wind — hoarsely & huskily through the leaves :
                        up & down
        dragging huskily through the shingle :
waves — huskily — over stones :
        drops         upon
    Rain∧snapping at the window-panes :

clicking gravel stones scud along the road :               10
sleet clicking against the pane :
waves snapping at the boulders : clashing
            clash of wind & water
waves : clashing against the stones : wind

slamming itself against houses, waves slam
            rain drops          ⎰
against cliff,∧ bang against ⎱cliff : leaves

clap ag together & ⎰wound each other : rumbling        15
                    ⎱against trunks
wind : shaking trees : drumming storm :

quavering breeze : buzzing rain (no wind)

whizzing hail : rustling flags : fizzing —
                              whooping⎰
gruff wind : screaming wind : yelling  ⎰ storm          19

tempest screeching over the hills, & yelling among trees ;

whining wind, wind piping its notes upon

the —— : groaning shore (waves against)

groaning waves, storm, wind : waves

snorting among the little caves of the shore

growling storm : snarling wind, shingle                    5

crying storm : the chime of insects (in
                                          birds & {insects
the wood)                                        {bees

    full band of $\frac{\text{birds}}{\text{insects}}$ : lamenting wind

strumming wind, rain : warbling wave


Aug. 9. Evening—candles lighted                    10

and the window left open—moths

enter from trees &c outside, hence

⟨    ⟩ in wood lighted ⟨        ⟩ or

any place with window open—

strange large moths & flies come                    15

in.

    ⟨    ⟩—Summer night—thunder

We cannot by an infinite ͵regress͵ discover .//.

demonstrations of demonstrations.　　F. Rewʷ

There was a man called Thorstein, the

son of Egil, &c. F. Revʷ ( ⌐ ᛩ ᐧ ᚵ ᒪ )

The Physiology of Thinking.　F. Revʷ　　　　　　5

the trumpet-call : acquired, then organised :

a system of words adopted ͵by convention͵ to represent .. :

outwardly the internal process of thinking :

parts of the nervous system, which undergo their

͵structural evolution͵ in a certain definite order :　　　10

motor processes : an almost automatic act :

Lamennais.　Contᵈ (F. Revʷ)

a social man .... ͵impassioned by͵ the highest

interests of society ... His immense need of

repose—such a need as is proper to great　　　　　15

natures ['proper' in Lat. sense] ... The passionate

limitation of view, & the ₍absoluteness of

expression₎ wh charᶻᵉ him : ... ₍Unfiguratively₎ ...

Lamennais was burdened with the melancholy

of one whose eye is fixed on great ideals ...

Indifference to religion ₍erected₎ itself into                    5

a doctrine [₍gathered itself into, cohered₎] ....

₍delivered₎ with precision [stated] ...


Pym. (Goldwin Smith.)

How natural to humanity, wearied

& perplexed with change, is this yearning           10

for the thrones & altars of the past!        2.

a compliant — a recusant.


In the same debate [on the petition of Right]

the courtiers prayed the House to ₍leave entire₎

his majesty's sovereign power. [leave entire the     15

perfect happˢ of the day — that his misery on that

subject shᵈ be left entire]

Mirabeau marked the intensity of conviction wh.

was to give ultimate ascendancy to the chief

of the Jacobins


'I have eaten the King's bread,' said Sir

Edmund Verney, the King's standard bearer,                    5

"near thirty years, & I will not do so base

a thing as to forsake him. I choose rather

to lose my life (which I am sure I shall do)

to preserve & defend those things wh are against

my conscience to preserve & defend; for I will              10

deal freely with you, I have no reverence for

the bishops, for whom this quarrel subsists.'

Sir Edmund's presentiment was true: the first

battle released him from this struggle between

his conscience & his chivalry.            17              15


Above all, the Commons had the lesser

gentry & the indepᵗ. yeomanry, everywhere attached

to the cause by its religious side. Those indep$^t$

yeom$^{y·}$ with high hearts & convictions of their own,

who filled the ranks of the Ironsides, who conq$^d$ for

Eng. lib. at Marston, Naseby & Worcester, in their

native England are seen no more. Here they have          5

left a great, pps a fatal gap, in the ranks of

freedom. But under Grant & Sherman they still

conquer for the good cause.                    17.

   Public virtue is not hereditary, & its

   titles ought not to be so              21.          10

   In that vast & sumptuous, but feebly con=

ceived & effeminately ornamented pile, no

unmeet shrine of Plutocracy, the present

House of Commons .. Pym is not.         22          14

        ———————///———————

The Saga of Gunnlaug the Worm Tongue & Rafn

the Skald. (F. Rev$^w$) He was nowise of such wondrous

growth & strength // as his father had been. ( ⌐⌐ ⁱᵒ ⟨⟩ )

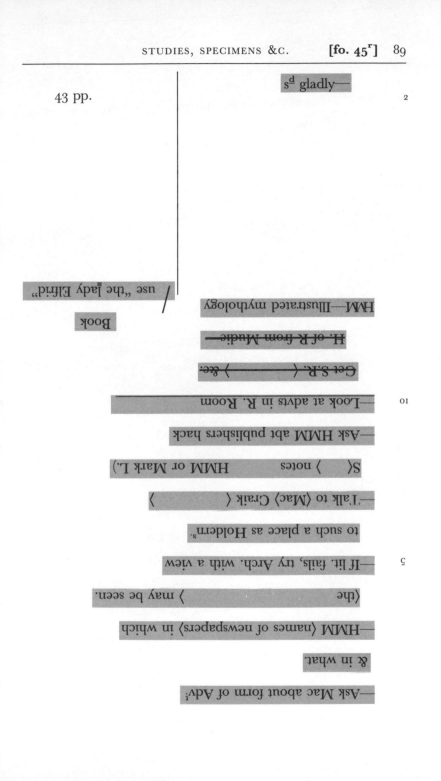

# Annotations

2.6–7 except . . . "——" · i.e. except phrases derived from biblical sources which are all additions except those within quotation marks.

3.1 Pre · i.e. private.

3.4 Shakesp · William Shakespeare. The references below are to volume, page, and line number of *The Dramatic Works of William Shakespeare*, ed. Samuel Weller Singer, 10 vols. (London: Bell and Daldy, 1856). TH's copy of this edition (DCM) has his signature in ink and '16 Westbourne Park Villas 1863—' in ink over erased pencil on the half-title of vol. I. Each of the volumes contains a few pencil markings and annotations. References in square brackets (act, scene, and line number) are to *The Riverside Shakespeare*, ed. G. Blakemore Evans (Boston: Houghton Mifflin, 1974).

3.5–7    It . . . they · *Cymbeline*, X.485.7–9 [V.v.215–17]: '. . . earth amend, | By . . .'.

3.8      Nor . . . cowardice · *Timon of Athens*, VIII.325.16 [III.v.16].

3.9–10   The hour . . . nine · *Timon*, VIII.320.7 [III.iv.8].

3.11     If . . . thee · *Timon*, VIII.328.23 [III.v.100]; cf. 9.2.

3.12     For . . . first · *Timon*, VIII.318.14 [III.iii.15]: 'But his . . .'.

3.14 Wordsworth · William Wordsworth. The references below are to stanza, line, and (in parentheses) page number of *The Poetical Works of William Wordsworth* (London: Routledge, Warne, & Routledge, 1864). TH's copy (DCM) has his signature in ink over pencil and address '16 Westbourne Park Villas' in pencil on the verso of the front endpaper. A few poems (e.g. 'Tintern Abbey', 'French Revolution') are extensively marked.

3.15     These all . . . me · 'Personal Talk', i.7 (182).

3.16     Square . . . desire · 'Personal Talk', i.10 (183).

3.17     its faint undersong · 'Personal Talk', i.14 (183).

3.17     flapping · 'Personal Talk', i.13 (183).

3.17     jibe · 'Personal Talk', ii.6 (183).

3.17     rancour · 'Personal Talk', iv.3 (183).

3.18     tarn · 'Fidelity', iii.4 (187); footnoted.

3.18     strains of rapture · 'The fairest, brightest hues of ether fade', 5 (190); cf. 20.8, 28.17.

3.19     the more . . . mind · 'Weak is the will of man, his judgment blind', 7 (191).

3.19     mutable · 'Hail Twilight, sovereign of one peaceful hour!', 4 (191).

4.1 Scott · Walter Scott. The references below are to stanza, line, and (in parentheses) page number of 'The Wild Huntsman', in *The Poetical Works of Sir Walter Scott*, ed. J. Logie Robertson, Oxford Complete Edition (London: Henry Frowde, 1904). The copy of *The Poetical Works of Sir Walter Scott, Bart.*

. . . *A New Edition, with Eight Illustrations by Corbould* (London: Routledge, Warne, & Routledge, 1863) now in the Beinecke certainly belonged to TH, but it seems not to have been the source of the entries in this notebook: it lacks, for example, some of Scott's final revisions and additions to his annotations, one of which is quoted by TH at 4.8–9.

4.1      the lated peasant · li.2 (637).

4.2      signs . . . cross · li.3 (637).

4.3 By · Lord Byron. The references below are to canto, stanza, line, and (in parentheses) page number of *Childe Harold's Pilgrimage*, in *Poems* (London: Routledge, Warne, & Routledge, 1864). TH's copy (Beinecke) contains his signature in ink on the title-page and numerous markings. There is an edition in DCM of *Childe Harold's Pilgrimage, The Prophecy of Dante, Beppo: A Venetian Story, and Fragments of an Incomplete Poem* (Halifax: Milner and Sowerby, 1865) with 'Hardy' written in ink on the half-title, but as this volume contains no markings all Byron references are to the Routledge edition.

4.3      grow . . . soil · I.xc.9 (531); although the phrase does not occur in Spenser's works, there are several references to 'native soyle': e.g. *The Faerie Queene* (see below, 4.12 n.), Book I, XI.ii.1 (109).

4.4      so . . . crest · I.xci.8 (532); cf. 58.1.

4.4      sable shore · II.viii.2 (534); cf. 6.19, 9.12.

4.5 Sc · Scott. The references below are to *Poetical Works* (see 4.1 n.).

4.5      O'er . . . hill · 'Wild Huntsman', xiii.2 (634).

4.5–6    with reverted eye · 'Wild Huntsman', xlix.1 (637): 'With wild despair's reverted eye'.

4.6      misbegotten · 'Wild Huntsman', xlvi.4 (636).

4.7      yawning rifts · 'Wild Huntsman', xlvi.2 (636).

4.7      tangled thorn · 'Wild Huntsman', xiv.1 (635).

4.7      rede · 'Wild Huntsman', xi.3 (634).

4.8      to rede · See preceding entry.

4.8–9    shagged with thorn · *The Lay of the Last Minstrel*, Note LIV (77), quoting John Leyden, *Scenes of Infancy*.

4.9      to speed · Perhaps *The Lord of the Isles*, V.xii.9 (453): 'God speed them!'

4.9      selle · *Lord of the Isles*, III.xxvi.13 (436) or VI.xiv.10 (464); cf. 6.10. As TH notes, the word (spelled 'sell') is also used by Spenser: e.g. *The Faerie Queene* (see below), Book II, II.xi.6 (144).

4.10–11  to hear . . . tell · 'Cadyow Castle', xlii.2 (669).

4.12 Spenser · Edmund Spenser. The references below are to book, canto, stanza, line, and (in parentheses) page number of *The Faerie Queene . . . to which is added his Epithalamion* (London: Routledge, Warne, & Routledge, 1865). TH's copy (DCM) has his signature and '16 Westbourne Pk Villas.' in ink on the title-page. There are a few markings in the volume.

4.12 sunny day · *Faerie Queene*, Book I, IV.viii.2 (33).

4.12     half loth · *Faerie Queene*, Book I, IV.xiv.1 (34); cf. 23.1.

4.12     middest · *Faerie Queene*, Book I, IV.xv.6 (34).

4.13     disspread · *Faerie Queene*, Book I, IV.xvii.9 (34): 'dispredden'; cf. 18.1.

4.13     mis-diet · *Faerie Queene*, Book I, IV.xxiii.8 (36).

4.13     to hurlten · *Faerie Queene*, Book I, IV.xl.1 (39): 'to hurtlen'.

4.13     aiding · 'Epithalamion', i.2 (793).

4.14     to neighbour · 'Epithalamion', iii.3 (793): 'neighbours'; cf. 10.10.

4.14     meeter · 'Epithalamion', v.13 (794).

4.14     unweeting · *Faerie Queene*, Book I, IV.xlvii.3 (40).

4.15 Shakes · Shakespeare. The references below are to *The Tempest*, in vol. I of *Dramatic Works*; those in square brackets are to *The Riverside Shakespeare* (see 3.4 n.). TH also owned a copy (DCM) of *The Tempest*, ed. John Hunter (London: Longmans, Green, and Co., n.d.), but it appears (from bound-in advertisements) to date from the 1880s rather than the 1860s and none of its occasional pencil markings coincide with the quotations in this notebook.

4.15     freshes · 57.28 [III.ii.67]; footnoted.

4.15     rootedly · 58.26 [III.ii.95].

4.16–17   Will . . . while-ere · 59.15–16 [III.ii.117–18]; cf. 7.7.

4.17     ladykin · 60.21 [III.iii.1]: 'lakin'; footnoted.

4.18 Sp · Spenser. The references below are to *The Faerie Queene*, Book I (see 4.12 n.).

4.18–19   Men . . . all · VII.xxxv.6–7 (70); cf. 5.18.

5.1      The iron . . . bit · VII.xxxvii.9 (70).

5.2      captived · VII.xxvi.9 (68).

5.2      thereto said he · IV.xlix.1 (41).

5.3      chase away sleep · IV.xliv.4 (40): 'chace away sweet sleepe'.

5.3      hoped victory · IV.xliv.5 (40).

5.4      I no whit reck · IV.l.9 (41); cf. 32.6, 59.10.

5.4      odds · IV.l.2 (41).

5.4–5    doughty tournament · V.i.7 (42).

5.5      oriental . . . heaven · V.ii.1–2 (42): '. . . Of greatest heaven'.

5.5–6    sunbright arms · V.ii.8 (42).

5.6      ruth · V.ix.7 (43); cf. 5.11.

5.6      her darksome mew · V.xx.4 (46); cf. 35.4.

5.7      where when she came · V.xlv.3 (51).

5.7–8    wretched thralls · V.xlv.9 (51).

5.8      Ind · VI.ii.7 (53).

5.8      looking lovely · VI.iv.2 (53).

5.9      ransack'd chastity · VI.v.5 (54).

5.9      piteous maiden · VI.vi.1 (54).

5.10     salvage · VI.xi.3 (55).

5.10–11   are won . . . ruth · VI.xii.7 (55): 'Are wonne with pitty . . .'; cf. 5.6.

5.11      an ivy twine · VI.xiv.9 (55).

5.11–12   Cybele's frantic rites · VI.xv.3 (56).

5.12      dryadés . . . hamad.ˢ · VI.xviii.1 (56): 'Hamadryades'.

5.13      naiadés · VI.xviii.3 (56).

5.13      timely · VI.xxiii.3 (57).

5.13      sturdy courage · VI.xxvi.8 (58).

5.13      behest · VI.xxvi.9 (58); cf. 12.7.

5.14      to weet of news · VI.xxxiv.5 (59); cf. 12.9.

5.14      Araby · VI.xxxv.6 (60).

5.15–16   The lesser . . . chief · VI.xxxvii.9 (60).

5.16      new breath'd · VI.xliv.9 (61).

5.16      leasing · VI.xlviii.1 (62).

5.17      with foul . . . fair · VII.iii.9 (63).

5.18      when him list · VII.xxxv.5 (70).

5.18      transmew · VII.xxxv.6 (70); cf. 4.18–19.

6.1 Words. · Wordsworth. The references below are to *Poetical Works* (see 3.14 n.).

6.2       fulgent · 'The shepherd, looking eastward, softly said', 5 (191).

6.2       trim array · 'Where lies the land to which yon ship must go?', 2 (192).

6.2       what boots it · 'Where lies the land', 5 (192): 'What boots the inquiry?'.

6.3       stress · 'Even as a dragon's eye that feels the stress', 1 (192).

6.3       bedimming · 'Even as a dragon's eye', 2 (192).

6.3       sepulchral · 'Even as a dragon's eye', 3 (192).

6.3–4     sky . . . clouds · 'Even as a dragon's eye', 6–7 (192).

6.4       imaging · Perhaps 'Mark the concentred hazels that inclose', 7 (193): 'The very image framing of a tomb'.

6.4–5     the wish'd-for · 'Composed after a Journey across the Hamilton Hills, Yorkshire', 2 (193).

6.5       to brood · 'These words were utter'd in a pensive mood', 5 (193): 'brood'.

6.5       chaplet · 'To the poet John Dyer', 7 (194).

6.6       one after one · 'To Sleep', 2 (195).

6.7–8 Sir W. S. Marmion c. 5 & 6 · Sir Walter Scott, *Marmion*, cantos 5 and 6. The references below are to *Poetical Works* (see 4.1 n.).

6.9       aright · *Marmion*, I.Introd.102 (90).

6.9       manned · *Marmion*, VI.ii.28 (155). For Scott's use of the word in TH's sense, however, see *The Lady of the Lake*, V.x.3 (253).

6.9     strook · *Marmion*, III.xiv.11 (118).

6.10    hostel · *Marmion*, III.xxvi.6 (122); also title of canto.

6.10    chapelle · *Marmion*, III.xxix.3 (123).

6.10    selle · *Marmion*, III.xxxi.10 (123); cf. 4.9.

6.11    wingèd · *Marmion*, IV.Introd.13 (124).

6.11    vext · *Marmion*, IV.Introd.35 (124).

6.11    donned · *Marmion*, IV.Introd.38 (124).

6.11    rack · *Marmion*, IV.Introd.42 (124).

6.12    dank · Not found; a typographical error in whatever edition of *Marmion* TH was using could conceivably have rendered as 'dank' one of the three occurrences of 'dark' in the second and third paragraphs of the Introduction to Canto IV.

6.12    mellowing · *Marmion*, IV.Introd.66 (124).

6.12    urn · *Marmion*, IV.Introd.138 (125).

6.12    to wake · *Marmion*, IV.Introd.148 (125): 'wake'.

6.13    kindly · *Marmion*, IV.Introd.153 (125).

6.13    laggard · *Marmion*, IV.Introd.189 (126).

6.13    mimosa · *Marmion*, IV.Introd.196 (126): 'Mimosa's'.

6.14    cap of maintenance · *Marmion*, IV.vii.12 (128).

6.15    meet time · *Marmion*, IV.viii.23 (129).

6.16    the steep · *Marmion*, IV.x.5 (129).

6.16    the eddy · *Marmion*, IV.x.8 (129): 'eddy'.

6.16    the mystic sense · *Marmion*, IV.xi.6 (129).

6.17    lordly · *Marmion*, IV.xi.11 (129).

6.17    laced · *Marmion*, IV.xi.13 (129).

6.17    cumber · *Marmion*, IV.xxi.32 (132).

6.18    had happed · *Marmion*, IV.xxii.3 (132); cf. 10.8.

6.18–19 Highland . . . plaid · *Marmion*, IV.xxii.11 (132).

6.19    sable pines · *Marmion*, IV.xxii.14 (132): 'sable pine-trees'; cf. 4.4, 9.12, 11.17.

6.19    trode · *Marmion*, IV.xxiii.2 (133).

7.1     whin · *Marmion*, IV.xxiv.2 (133).

7.1     breezes thin · *Marmion*, IV.xxiv.5 (133).

7.1     I ween · *Marmion*, IV.xxv.8 (133).

7.2     vassal-rank · *Marmion*, IV.xxvi.10 (133).

7.2     pavillion · *Marmion*, IV.xxviii.7 (134): 'pavilions'.

7.3     the ruddy . . . gold · *Marmion*, IV.xxviii.18 (134).

7.4     the whilst · *Marmion*, IV.xxxi.9 (135).

7.4     leagured · *Marmion*, IV.xxxii.14 (135).

7.4     'gainst · *Marmion*, IV.xxxii.13 (135).

7.4     larum · *Marmion*, IV.xxxii.11 (135).

7.5       inveighs ag$^{st}$ · *Marmion*, V.Introd.24 (136).

7.5       riven · *Marmion*, V.Introd.35 (136).

7.5       umbered · *Marmion*, V.Introd.58 (136).

7.6       corslet · *Marmion*, V.Introd.69 (136): 'corslet's'.

7.6       paly · *Marmion*, V.Introd.74 (136).

7.6       whilome · *Marmion*, V.Introd.75 (137); cf. 8.6.

7.7       matchless · *Marmion*, V.Introd.76 (137).

7.7       whilere · *Marmion*, V.Introd.139 (137); cf. 4.17.

7.7-8     Toledo blade · *Marmion*, V.viii.17 (141): 'blade, Toledo right'.

7.8       a minstrel's malison · *Marmion*, V.xxv.9 (148).

7.9       gibber · *Marmion*, V.xxv.14 (148).

7.9-10    Wh of . . . fall · *The Bridal of Triermain*, I.iv.1-3 (556): 'which of ye all . . .'

7.10-13   the torrent . . . flung · *The Vision of Don Roderick*, I.iv.3, 5-6 (591): 'Ye torrents . . .'; 'maj$^{c}$' = 'majestic'.

7.13      trumpet-jubilee · *Don Roderick*, I.v.4 (591).

7.14      tincture · *Rokeby*, I.i.4 (313).

7.14-15   like . . . glow · *Rokeby*, I.i.12 (313).

7.15      sorrow's livery · *Rokeby*, I.i.13 (313).

7.15      yare · *Marmion*, I.ix.8 (95).

7.16 Shakes · Shakespeare. The references below are to *Pericles*, in vol. IV of *Dramatic Works*; those in square brackets are to *The Riverside Shakespeare* (see 3.4 n.).

7.16-17   Praises . . . given · 209.3-4 [IV.Cho.34-5]; line in margin.

7.17-18   Paragon . . . reports · 212.11 [IV.i.35]; footnoted.

7.18      that he . . . descrip$^{n}$ · 218.31-2 [IV.ii.100-1]; shorthand = 'went to bed to her'.

8.1 Var$^{s.}$ · Presumably an abbreviation for 'Various', indicating that the listed words derive from a variety of sources not specifically noted or recollected (cf. 'Recoll' at 22.2 and n.). Most of them can in fact be found either in Shakespeare or in Scott—'marge' and 'whilome', indeed, are quoted from *The Tempest* and *Marmion*, respectively, elsewhere in the notebook (at 14.14 and 7.6)—and some (e.g. 'athwart', 'sere', 'anon') appear in both. In several instances it would be possible to suggest a range of sources which TH might have known or consulted—'it irks me', for instance, might have derived from *As You Like It*, from Byron's *The Corsair*, or from common speech—but 'better hand', as meaning 'right hand', is not recorded at all in *OED*, although it does appear in Joseph Wright's *English Dialect Dictionary*. Cf. 'tense' at 54.15, 'serest' at 14.12, and 'to glean' at 33.5.

8.8 Gol. Trea · *The Golden Treasury of the Best Songs and Lyrical Poems in the English Language*. The references below are to stanza, line, and (in parentheses) page number of the first edition, ed. Francis Turner Palgrave (Cambridge: Macmillan, 1861). TH's copy (DCM) is inscribed in ink on the verso of the front endpaper: 'T. Hardy | from | H M Moule | Jan. 1862'. The volume contains numerous markings, chiefly erased underlinings of individual words, and some annotations.

8.8      palm · T. Nash [Thomas Nashe], 'Spring' ['Song': 'Spring, the sweet spring', from *Summer's Last Will and Testament*], 5 (1); underlined (erased).

8.8      decore · W. Drummond of Hawthornden [William Drummond of Hawthornden], 'Summons to Love' ['Song ii': 'Phoebus arise'], 11 (2); underlined (erased).

8.9      diadem of pearl · Drummond, 'Summons to Love' ['Phoebus arise'], 12 (2); underlined (erased).

8.9      frisk · Nashe, 'Spring', 6 (1).

8.9–10      blushing beams · Drummond, 'Summons to Love' ['Phoebus arise'], 25 (2); underlined (erased).

8.10      did . . . surprise · Drummond, 'Summons to Love' ['Phoebus arise'], 28 (2); 'thy heart surprise' underlined (erased).

8.11      pipe all day · Nashe, 'Spring', 6 (1); underlined (erased).

8.11      sunning · Nashe, 'Spring', 10 (1); underlined (erased).

8.11–12      tune . . . lay · Nashe, 'Spring', 7 (1); 'merry lay' underlined (erased).

8.12      purely white · Drummond, 'Summons to Love' ['Phoebus arise'], 20 (2).

8.12      ivybuds · C. Marlowe [Christopher Marlowe], 'The Passionate Shepherd to His Love', v.1 (4); underlined (erased).

8.13      deck . . . guise · Drummond, 'Summons to Love' ['Phoebus arise'], 29 (2); 'deck' underlined (erased).

8.13–15      the clouds . . . blue · Drummond, 'Summons to Love' ['Phoebus arise'], 42 (2); 'orient' and 'spangle' underlined (erased). Cf. 10.13.

8.15      stud · Marlowe, 'Passionate Shepherd', v.2 (4): 'studs'.

8.15      honey breath · Shakespeare, 'Time and Love 2' [Sonnet 65], 5 (3); underlined (erased).

8.15–16      Time's best jewel · Shakespeare, 'Time and Love 2' [Sonnet 65], 10 (3).

8.16–17      melodious . . . madrigals · Marlowe, 'Passionate Shepherd', ii.4 (4); 'Melodious' underlined (erased).

8.17      falls · Marlowe, 'Passionate Shepherd', ii.3 (4).

8.17      carol · Shakespeare, 'It was a lover and his lass' [*As You Like It*, V.iii.16–33], 9 (6); underlined (erased).

8.18      enjoy . . . her · Anon., 'Present in Absence' ['Absence, hear thou my protestation', from Francis Davison's *A Poetical Rhapsody*], iii.6 (7); underlined (erased).

8.18–9.1      teeming . . . increase · Shakespeare, 'How like a winter hath my absence been' [Sonnet 97], 6 (7); underlined (erased).

9.1    my rose, thou · Shakespeare, 'The Unchangeable' [Sonnet 109], 14
       (9): 'Save thou, my rose'.

9.2    three summer's pride · Shakespeare, 'To me, fair Friend, you
       never can be old' [Sonnet 104], 4 (9): 'Three summers' pride';
       'pride' underlined (erased); cf. 3.11.

9.3    sweet hue · Shakespeare, 'To me, fair Friend' [Sonnet 104], 11 (9).

9.3    I do love thee · H. Constable [Henry Constable], 'Diaphenia', i.4
       (9).

9.3    sweets · Constable, 'Diaphenia', ii.2 (10); line in margin (erased); cf.
       62.2, 62.12.

9.4    dear joy (thee) · Constable, 'Diaphenia', iii.3 (10): 'Dear joy, how I
       do love thee!'; 'Dear joy' underlined (erased).

9.4    twines · T. Lodge [Thomas Lodge], 'Rosaline' ['Rosalynde's
       Description', from Rosalynde: Euphues Golden Legacie], i.4 (10).

9.5    sapphires . . . snow · Lodge, 'Rosaline' ['Rosalynde's Description'],
       i.6 (10).

9.5    blushing cloud · Lodge, 'Rosaline' ['Rosalynde's Description'], ii.1
       (10).

9.6    sting · Nashe, 'Spring', 3 (1); underlined (erased).

9.6    your furious . . . stay · Drummond, 'Summons to Love' ['Phoebus
       arise'], 32 (2); 'furious chiding' underlined (erased).

9.7    fell hand · Shakespeare, 'Time and Love 1' [Sonnet 64], 1 (3): 'fell'
       underlined (erased).

9.7    alack · Shakespeare, 'Time and Love 2' [Sonnet 65], 9 (3).

9.7    bare · Shakespeare, 'A Madrigal' [The Passionate Pilgrim, XII], 8 (5).

9.7–8  freezings . . . felt · Shakespeare, 'How like a winter' [Sonnet 97] 3
       (7); 'freezings' underlined (erased).

9.8    beweep · Shakespeare, 'A Consolation' [Sonnet 29], 2 (8); under-
       lined (erased).

9.8    bootless · Shakespeare, 'A Consolation' [Sonnet 29], 3 (8); under-
       lined (erased).

9.9    sullen earth · Shakespeare, 'A Consolation' [Sonnet 29], 12 (8);
       'sullen' underlined (erased).

9.9–11 Ah . . . perceived · Shakespeare, 'To me, fair Friend' [Sonnet
       104], 9–10 (9); 'Steal from his figure' underlined (erased).

9.11–12 paint . . . skies · Drummond, 'Summons to Love' ['Phoebus
       arise'], 2 (1); 'paint' underlined (erased). Cf. 4.4, 6.19.

9.12   rouse · Drummond, 'Summons to Love' ['Phoebus arise'], 4 (1).

9.12   career · Drummond, 'Summons to Love' ['Phoebus arise'], 5 (2);
       underlined (erased).

9.13   wont · Drummond, 'Summons to Love' ['Phoebus arise'], 10 (2);
       cf. 13.10.

9.13    chase hence · Drummond, 'Summons to Love' ['Phoebus arise'], 13 (2); 'Chase' underlined (erased).

9.13    sworn · Drummond, 'Summons to Love' ['Phoebus arise'], 18 (2).

9.14    tarry · Anon., 'Present in Absence' ['Absence'], ii.6 (6).

9.14    makes vanish · Drummond, 'Summons to Love' ['Phoebus arise'], 38 (2).

9.14    reels · Drummond, 'Summons to Love' ['Phoebus arise'], 39 (2).

9.15    shun · Drummond, 'Summons to Love' ['Phoebus arise'], 40 (2).

9.15    outworn buried age · Shakespeare, 'Time and Love 1' [Sonnet 64], 2 (3); 'out-worn' underlined (erased).

9.15–16  buried age · See preceding entry.

9.16    razed · Shakespeare, 'Time and Love 1' [Sonnet 64], 3 (3): 'down-razed'.

9.16    confounded · Shakespeare, 'Time and Love 1' [Sonnet 64], 10 (3).

9.17    o'ersways · Shakespeare, 'Time and Love 2' [Sonnet 65], 2 (3); underlined (erased).

9.17    plea · Shakespeare, 'Time and Love 2' [Sonnet 65], 3 (3); underlined (erased).

9.17    battering days · Shakespeare, 'Time and Love 2' [Sonnet 65], 6 (3); underlined (erased).

9.18    prime · Shakespeare, 'It was a lover and his lass', 13 (6).

9.18    spoil of beauty · Shakespeare, 'Time and Love 2' [Sonnet 65], 12 (3).

9.18–19  craggy mountains · Marlowe, 'Passionate Shepherd', i.4 (4); 'craggy' underlined (erased).

9.19    kirtle · Marlowe, 'Passionate Shepherd', iii.3 (4); underlined (erased).

9.19    nimble · Shakespeare, 'A Madrigal' [*Passionate Pilgrim*, XII], 11 (5); underlined (erased).

9.19    hie · Shakespeare, 'A Madrigal' [*Passionate Pilgrim*, XII], 19 (5).

10.1    defy · Shakespeare, 'A Madrigal' [*Passionate Pilgrim*, XII], 18 (5).

10.1    folks · Shakespeare, 'It was a lover and his lass', 8 (6).

10.1    crowned · Shakespeare, 'It was a lover and his lass', 13 (6).

10.1–2  truest mettle · Anon., 'Present in Absence' ['Absence'], i.5 (6).

10.2    vary · Anon., 'Present in Absence' ['Absence'], ii.5 (6).

10.2    tend · Shakespeare, 'Absence' [Sonnet 57], 1 (7).

10.2    bid · Shakespeare, 'Absence' [Sonnet 57], 8 (7).

10.3    fleeting · Shakespeare, 'How like a winter' [Sonnet 97], 2 (7); underlined (erased); cf. 72.17.

10.3    old December · Shakespeare, 'How like a winter' [Sonnet 97], 4 (7): 'old December's'.

10.3          mute · Shakespeare, 'How like a winter' [Sonnet 97], 12 (8).

10.4          featured like · Shakespeare, 'A Consolation' [Sonnet 29], 6 (8); underlined (erased).

10.4          that man's scope · Shakespeare, 'A Consolation' [Sonnet 29], 7 (8); 'scope' underlined (erased).

10.5          scorn to · Shakespeare, 'A Consolation' [Sonnet 29], 14 (8).

10.5          ranged · Shakespeare, 'The Unchangeable' [Sonnet 109], 5 (8); underlined (erased). Cf. 20.14–15.

10.5–7        All . . . blood · Shakespeare, 'The Unchangeable' [Sonnet 109], 10 (9); line in margin (erased) and 'besiege' underlined (erased).

10.7          sum of good · Shakespeare, 'The Unchangeable' [Sonnet 109], 12 (9); 'sum' underlined (erased).

10.7          prove me · Constable, 'Diaphenia', i.6 (9).

10.8          selfsame · Lodge, 'Rosaline' ['Rosalynde's Description'], i.3 (10).

10.8          aye · Nashe, 'Spring', 7 (1); underlined (erased).

10.8          happed · See next entry; cf. 6.18.

10.8          haply · Shakespeare, 'A Consolation' [Sonnet 29], 10 (8).

10.9–11       her lips . . . nigh · Lodge, 'Rosaline' ['Rosalynde's Description'], ii.6–7 (10); cf. 4.14.

10.11         centres of delight · Lodge, 'Rosaline' ['Rosalynde's Description'], iii.6 (11).

10.11         orbs · Lodge, 'Rosaline' ['Rosalynde's Description'], iii.7 (11); cf. 18.13.

10.12         feed perfection · Lodge, 'Rosaline' ['Rosalynde's Description'], iii.9 (11).

10.13–16      with orient . . . view · Lodge, 'Rosaline' ['Rosalynde's Description'], iv.1–4 (11): 'With orient pearl, with ruby red, | With marble white, with sapphire blue | Her body . . .'; cf. 8.14.

10.17         nymphs · Lodge, 'Rosaline' ['Rosalynde's Description'], v.1 (11).

10.17         calm · The Shepherd Tonie [Anthony Munday], 'Colin' ['To Colin Cloute': 'Beauty sat bathing by a spring'], i.3 (11).

10.17         darling buds · Shakespeare, 'To His Love' [Sonnet 18], 3 (12).

10.17–18      every . . . declines · Shakespeare, 'To His Love' [Sonnet 18], 7 (12): '. . . sometime declines'; cf. 11.11.

10.19         beauty making beautiful · Shakespeare, 'To His Love' [Sonnet 106], 3 (12).

10.19         beauty's best · Shakespeare, 'To His Love' [Sonnet 106], 5 (13).

11.1          passing fair · Shakespeare, 'Love's Perjuries' [*Passionate Pilgrim*, XVI], 3 (13).

11.1–2        Love . . . May · Shakespeare, 'Love's Perjuries' [*Passionate Pilgrim*, XVI], 2 (13).

11.2          velvet leaves · Shakespeare, 'Love's Perjuries' [*Passionate Pilgrim*, XVI], 5 (13).

11.2        fondle · Apparently A. Philips [Ambrose Philips], 'To Charlotte
            Pulteney', 2 (111): 'Fondling'.

11.3        bemoan · Lodge, 'Rosaline' ['Rosalynde's Description'], v.1 (11).

11.3        chidden · The Shepherd Tonie, 'Colin' ['Beauty sat bathing'], i.8
            (11).

11.3        dimm'd · Shakespeare, 'To His Love' [Sonnet 18], 6 (12); cf.
            36.4.

11.3        brand · Lodge, 'Rosaline' ['Rosalynde's Description'], iv.9 (11).

11.4        mischanced · W. Alexander, Earl of Sterline [Sir William
            Alexander, Earl of Stirling], 'To Aurora' [*Aurora*, Sonnet 33: 'O if
            thou knew'st how thou thyself dost harm'], 10 (15).

11.4        apt to entice · Lodge, 'Rosaline' ['Rosalynde's Description'], ii.9
            (10).

11.4        imprisoned · Lodge, 'Rosaline' ['Rosalynde's Description'], iii.2
            (10).

11.6        moulds · Lodge, 'Rosaline' ['Rosalynde's Description'], iii.8 (11);
            cf. 26.3.

11.6        muse not · Lodge, 'Rosaline' ['Rosalynde's Description'], v.1 (11).

11.6        spied · Shakespeare, 'Love's Perjuries' [*Passionate Pilgrim*, XVI], 3
            (13).

11.7        wasted time · Shakespeare, 'To His Love' [Sonnet 106], 1 (12).

11.7        blazon · Shakespeare, 'To His Love' [Sonnet 106], 5 (13).

11.8        lack · Shakespeare, 'To His Love' [Sonnet 106], 14 (13).

11.8        prefiguring · Shakespeare, 'To His Love' [Sonnet 106], 10 (13).

11.8        divining eyes · Shakespeare, 'To His Love' [Sonnet 106], 11 (13).

11.9        unmeet · Shakespeare, 'Love's Perjuries' [*Passionate Pilgrim*, XVI],
            13 (13).

11.9–10     deny . . . Jove · Shakespeare, 'Love's Perjuries' [*Passionate Pilgrim*,
            XVI], 19 (13).

11.10       intent · Sir T. Wyat [Sir Thomas Wyatt], 'A Supplication'
            ['Forget not yet'], i.1 (14).

11.10       travail · Wyatt, 'A Supplication' ['Forget not yet'], i.3 (14).

11.10       assays · Wyatt, 'A Supplication' ['Forget not yet'], iii.1 (14).

11.11       amiss · Wyatt, 'A Supplication' ['Forget not yet'], iv.3 (14).

11.11       riot · Not found in the *Golden Treasury*.

11.11       sometime · Shakespeare, 'To His Love' [Sonnet 18], 7 (12); cf.
            10.17–18, 15.6, 50.17.

11.11       'gan · Shakespeare, 'Love's Perjuries' [*Passionate Pilgrim*, XVI], 6
            (13).

11.12 Shelley · Percy Bysshe Shelley. The references below are to canto,
stanza, line, and (in parentheses) page number of *The Revolt of Islam*, in *Queen
Mab, and Other Poems* (Halifax: Milner and Sowerby, 1865). TH's copy
(Adams) has his signature and '16 Westbourne Park Villas 1866' in ink on

the half-title and a second signature in ink on the title-page; *The Revolt of Islam* and *Prometheus Unbound* are extensively marked and occasionally annotated.

11.12      the blast · III.xii.6 (125); cf. 18.2.

11.12      strip me stark · III.xiii.3 (125).

11.13      bare · III.xiii.4 (125).

11.13      beamless & pallid · III.xiii.9 (125).

11.13      circling sea · III.xv.2 (125).

11.14      silentness · III.xv.3 (125).

11.14      topmost · III.xvi.2 (126); cf. 25.10.

11.14      its sails were flagging · III.xvii.13 (126).

11.15      tameless resolve · III.xix.7 (127); cf. 48.10, 48.13.

11.15      linked remembrance · III.xix.8 (127).

11.16      methought · III.xxv.1 (128).

11.16–17   when low . . . pines · III.xxviii.7–8 (129); cf. 6.19.

11.17      infold · III.xxix.4 (129).

11.17      tranced · Perhaps suggested by III.xxx.9 (130): 'In trance had lain me thus', although 'tranced' itself occurs at V.xvii.1 (146).

11.18      wildering · III.xxxiii.2 (130).

11.18      joyance · III.viii.2 (123).

11.18      darkness was piled · III.xxxiii.9 (131): 'darkness again was piled'.

11.19      wove a shade · III.xxxiv.9 (131): 'a shade under the starlight wove'.

11.19      did flee · III.xxxiv.7 (131).

12.1 Byron · The references below are to *Childe Harold's Pilgrimage*, in *Poems* (see 4.3 n.).

12.1       harp . . . string · I.xiii.2 (512).

12.1       albeit · I.xiii.3 (512); cf. 15.10.

12.2       fellest · I.xv.9 (514).

12.2       whereon · I.xvi.4 (515); cf. 17.3.

12.3 Shakes · Shakespeare. The references below are to *The Tempest*, in vol. I of *Dramatic Works*; those in square brackets are to *The Riverside Shakespeare* (see 3.4 n.).

12.3–4     cram . . . ears · 34.20 [II.i.107]: 'cram these words . . .'.

12.4       rate · 34.23 [II.i.110].

12.4       weighed between · 35.9 [II.i.131]; footnoted.

12.5       escape · 35.25 [II.i.147].

12.6       tilth · 36.5 [II.i.153].

12.6       nimble lungs · 37.7 [II.i.174].

12.7       hest · 53.3 [III.i.37]; footnoted. Cf. 5.13.

12.7       skill-less · 53.19 [III.i.53].

12.8        totters · 55.20 [III.ii.7].

12.8        marmozet · 49.31 [II.ii.170].

12.9 Shell · Shelley. The references below are to *The Revolt of Islam*, in *Queen Mab, and Other Poems* (see 11.12 n.).

12.9        mailed against · IV.xix.7 (136): "Gainst scorn, and death and pain thus trebly mailed'; cf. 16.4.

12.9        he inly weets · IV.xiv.5 (135); cf. 5.14.

12.10       swart · Perhaps III.xxv.5 (128): 'swarthy'. TH would have found the spelling 'swart' in *Hellas* (not in the *Queen Mab* volume), 383, or in Scott's *The Vision of Don Roderick* (see next entry), II.liii.4 (603).

12.10       countered · Not found in Shelley; it does, however, appear in Scott's *Rokeby* (see next entry), III.x.9 (336).

12.11 Scott · The references below are to *Poetical Works* (see 4.1 n.).

12.11       glozed upon · *Rokeby*, I.xi.1 (316).

12.12       On the . . . placed · *Marmion*, II.i.19–20 (104).

12.13       heirs · *Rokeby*, I.xxi.16 (320).

12.13–14    when . . . wish · *Rokeby*, I.xxi.33 (320).

12.14       begirdled · *Rokeby*, II.i.13 (324): 'rock-begirdled'.

12.14–15    and dew the woods · *Rokeby*, II.ii.10 (324).

12.15       Staindrop . . . salutes · *Rokeby*, II.iii.5–6 (324): 'Staindrop, who, . . . Salutes'.

12.16       pouring a lay · *Rokeby*, II.iii.28 (324); cf. 14.19–15.1.

12.16       dimwood · *Rokeby*, II.iii.15 (324).

12.16–18    Knitting . . . land · *Rokeby*, II.iii.29–30 (324).

12.18       in the dawning seen · *Rokeby*, II.vi.3 (325).

12.19       spires · *Rokeby*, II.viii.11 (326).

12.19       grisly · *Rokeby*, II.x.3 (326).

13.1        in his despite · *Rokeby*, II.xix.12 (329).

13.1–2      pull'd . . . brambles · *Rokeby*, III.xiv.3–4 (337); cf. 13.19, 40.1.

13.2–3      tuck of drum · *Rokeby*, III.xvii.16 (338).

13.3        I . . . dragoon · *Rokeby*, III.xvii.15 (338); cf. 14.16, 35.8.

13.4        teach a tale · Perhaps suggested by *Rokeby*, III.xix.1 (338): 'his wondrous tale he told'; cf. also next entry.

13.5        tale of eld · *Rokeby*, III.xix.6 (338): 'tales of eld'.

13.5        spell · *Rokeby*, III.xix.10 (338); cf. 14.16, 41.17.

13.5        ban dog · *Rokeby*, III.xix.15 (339).

13.6        submiss(ve) · *Rokeby*, III.xxi.6 (339): 'Submiss'.

13.6–7      when . . . embrowned · *Rokeby*, III.xxi.17 (339).

13.7–8      nor . . . untwine · *Rokeby*, III.xxii.15–16 (339); 'c^{d}' = 'could'.

13.8–9      to wot so well · *Rokeby*, III.xxiv.2 (340).

13.9–10      aught . . . rare · *Rokeby*, III.xxiv.17 (340).

13.10        I . . . wont · *Rokeby*, III.xxv.11 (340); cf. 9.13.

13.10        to blench · *Rokeby*, III.xxvii.7 (341): 'blench'.

13.11        our hardiest venture · *Rokeby*, III.xxvii.9 (341).

13.11        spial · *Rokeby*, III.xxvii.23 (341).

13.12        sally port · *Rokeby*, III.xxvii.25 (341).

13.12        fair · *Rokeby*, III.xxvii.24 (341).

13.12        roundelay · *Rokeby*, III.xxviii.6 (341).

13.13        I trow · *Rokeby*, III.xxviii.17 (341).

13.13–14     some . . . heart · *Rokeby*, III.xxix.11 (341).

13.14        centred in · *Rokeby*, III.xxix.8 (341): 'centred all in'.

13.14–15     Allan-a-Dale . . . knight · *Rokeby*, III.xxx.13 (342).

13.15–16     to lodge the deer · *Rokeby*, III.xxxi.9 (342): 'lodged our deer'.

13.16–17     to pitch . . . net · *Rokeby*, III.xxxi.17 (342).

13.17        garth · *Rokeby*, IV.i.13 (343).

13.17–18     thy desperate quest · *Rokeby*, IV.iv.8 (344); cf. 15.13.

13.18        azure pencilled flower · *Rokeby*, IV.ii.21 (343).

13.19        festal time · *Rokeby*, IV.v.30 (344); cf. 33.7.

13.19        wilding · *Rokeby*, IV.xii.1 (346); cf. 13.2.

14.1         and down . . . hail · *Rokeby*, IV.xii.13 (346).

14.2         on upland fades · *Rokeby*, V.ii.1 (353).

14.2         this helpless fair · *Rokeby*, V.v.26 (354).

14.3         the tale goes · *Rokeby*, V.ix.27–8 (356).

14.3         a ring . . . kerne · *Rokeby*, V.x.13 (356).

14.4         in this bound · *Rokeby*, V.xi.9 (356): 'in this calm domestic bound'.

14.4         prone · *Rokeby*, V.xviii.4 (359).

14.4         reared · *Rokeby*, V.xxiii.21 (361).

14.5         taxing his fancy · *Rokeby*, V.xxv.21 (361).

14.5         dally not · *Rokeby*, V.xxix.10 (363).

14.6         prore · *Rokeby*, VI.xviii.25 (372).

14.6         according · *The Lady of the Lake*, I[Prologue].14 (207).

14.7         heathery · *Lady of the Lake*, I.ii.4 (208).

14.7         bold burst · *Lady of the Lake*, I.iv.12 (208).

14.8         lave · *Lady of the Lake*, I.xv.13 (211).

14.8         emprise · *Lady of the Lake*, I.xxiv.5 (214).

14.8–9       the guardian . . . chid · *Lady of the Lake*, II.vi.16 (219).

14.9         more . . . louder · *Lady of the Lake*, II.xvii.1–2 (222).

14.10        pipe music · A reference to the source of the sound described in the preceding entry.

14.10      amain · *Lady of the Lake*, II.xvii.22 (222).

14.10      foreshow · *Lady of the Lake*, II.xxxi.16 (227).

14.11      to ban · *Lady of the Lake*, III.vii.29 (231): 'to bless or ban'.

14.11      doom . . . woe · *Lady of the Lake*, III.ix.10 (232).

14.12      serest · *Lady of the Lake*, III.xvi.14 (234); cf. 8.5.

14.12      font · *Lady of the Lake*, III.xvi.5 (234).

14.12      bristles · *Lady of the Lake*, III.xvii.5 (234).

14.13 Shak · Shakespeare. The references below are to *Dramatic Works*; those in square brackets are to *The Riverside Shakespeare* (see 3.4 n.).

14.13      twink · *Tempest*, I.68.2 [IV.i.43].

14.13      brims · *Tempest*, I.69.1 [IV.i.64].

14.14      marge · *Tempest*, I.69.6 [IV.i.69]: 'sea-marge'; cf. 8.4.

14.14–15   thyself dost air · *Tempest*, I.69.7 [IV.i.70].

14.15      scarf · *Tempest*, I.69.19 [IV.i.82].

14.15      opposing · *Pericles*, IV.192.6 [III.Cho.17].

14.16 Sc · Scott. The references below are to *Poetical Works* (see 4.1 n.).

14.16      tell · *The Bridal of Triermain*, Introd.iv.10 (554).

14.16      guess · *Bridal*, Introd.iv.6 (554): 'guess'd'.

14.16      spell · *Bridal*, Introd.iv.9 (554); cf. 13.5, 41.17.

14.16      bode · *Bridal*, I.vi.23 (556).

14.16      read · *Rokeby*, III.xvii.15 (338); cf. 13.3, 35.8.

14.16      trace · *Bridal*, I.vi.19 (556).

14.17      troth · *Bridal*, II.xvii.5 (565).

14.17      paled in · *Bridal*, Introd.iii.2 (553) or I.xiii.1 (558).

14.17–18   months . . . flown · *Bridal*, II.vi.1 (562).

14.18      stolen-wise · *Bridal*, II.xiii.21 (564).

14.18–19   well-a-day · *The Lay of the Last Minstrel*, Introd.9 (1).

14.19      their . . . fled · *Lay*, Introd.9 (1).

14.19–15.1 poured the lay · *Lay*, Introd.17–18 (1): 'pour'd to lord and lady gay | The unpremeditated lay'; cf. 12.16.

15.1       wight · *Lay*, I.v.3 (3) or *Bridal*, II.xvi.11 (564).

15.1       coined . . . empery · *Bridal*, III.xxv.12 (579).

15.2 Jean I. · Jean Ingelow. The references below are to stanza, line, and (in parentheses) page number in *Poems* (London: Longman, Green, Longman, Roberts, & Green, 1863).

15.2–3     It was . . . reverie · 'The Letter L. Absent', xv.1–2 (111).

15.3–4     like roses blown · 'Letter L. Absent', xiv.2 (111).

15.4       in loving wise · 'Letter L. Absent', xvi.3 (111).

15.4       bide · 'Letter L. Absent', xxxi.4 (114).

15.4       blue bergs · 'Letter L. Absent', xxxv.4 (115).

15.5     navigate . . . main · 'Letter L. Absent', xxxvi.2 (115); cf. 17.14.

15.5     vagrant · 'Letter L. Absent', xxxvii.1 (115).

15.6     fancy fraught · 'Letter L. Absent', xli.4 (116).

15.6     my sometime pride · 'Letter L. Absent', xliv.1 (116); cf. 11.11, 50.17–18.

15.7     my heart within · 'Letter L. Absent', xlvii.4 (117).

15.7     wis · 'Letter L. Absent', liii.3 (118).

15.8–9   who find . . . akin · 'Letter L. Absent', lv.3 (118): '. . . not ought thereto . . .' (where 'aught', used in the 1867 edition of *Poems*, is clearly correct).

15.9     to brim · 'Letter L. Absent', lxv.3 (120): 'brim'.

15.9     whelmed · 'Letter L. Absent', lxxiii.3 (121).

15.10    albeit · 'Letter L. Absent', lxxx.3 (122); cf. 12.1.

15.10    lithe & tall · 'Letter L. Absent', lxxix.3 (122); cf. 66.6.

15.11    tendance · 'Letter L. Absent', xciii.4 (124).

15.11–12 the little . . . No · 'Letter L. Absent', xcviii.3–4 (125).

15.12    forecasting · 'The Letter L. Present', lii.1 (134).

15.13    a quest · 'Letter L. Present', lvii.4 (135): 'her quest'; cf. 13.18.

15.14    waxing life · 'Letter L. Present', lix.3 (135).

15.14–16 He would . . . eternally · 'Letter L. Present', lx.1–4 (136): '. . . fain | (One morning on the halcyon sea) | That life . . .'; cf. 29.10, 49.13.

15.16    let fall · 'Letter L. Present', lix.1 (135).

15.16–17 flusheth . . . favour · 'Divided', I.iii.1 (1).

15.18    to prank · 'Divided', I.iv.4 (1).

15.19    beck · 'Divided', II.ii.4 (2).

15.19    westering · 'Divided', II.iv.4 (2).

15.20 southing, northing · Neither of these forms has been traced in Chaucer's works, nor does *OED* give any citations earlier than the mid-seventeenth century.

16.1 Shak · Shakespeare. The reference below is to *Henry IV. Part I*, in vol. V of *Dramatic Works*; that in square brackets is to *The Riverside Shakespeare* (see 3.4 n.).

16.1     so he · 23.18 [I.iii.76].

16.2 Shell · Shelley. The references below are to *The Revolt of Islam*, in *Queen Mab, and Other Poems* (see 11.12 n.).

16.2     utmost · V.i.1 (141); cf. 19.18.

16.2–3   a might . . . thought · V.ii.4–5 (141); line in margin.

16.3–4   cradled . . . night · V.ii.5 (141); line in margin.

16.4     in woven . . . mailed · V.ii.8 (141); line in margin. Cf. 12.9.

16.4–5   our mingling . . . brooded · V.v.9 (142).

16.5      outspring · V.vi.5 (142): 'outsprung'.

16.6      scare · V.vii.7 (143).

16.6–7    smiles . . . balm · V.x.5–6 (144).

16.7–8    a film . . . dimness · V.xii.3–4 (144).

16.8      kingly · V.xiv.7 (145); cf. 48.9.

16.8      giddy turret · V.xv.2 (145).

16.9      idle winds · V.xv.4 (145).

16.9      spire . . . sky · V.xv.3 (145); cf. 25.8.

16.10     flower-inwoven crowns · V.xvi.6 (145).

16.10     token flowers · V.xvi.7 (145).

16.11     to lead a dance · V.xxi.1–2 (147): 'led before him | A graceful dance'.

16.11     a rainbow, braided · V.xxiv.1 (148).

16.12 Skak · i.e. 'Shak', for Shakespeare. The references below are to *Henry IV. Part I*, in vol. V of *Dramatic Works*; those in square brackets are to *The Riverside Shakespeare* (see 3.4 n.).

16.12     tristful · 64.9 [II.iv.393].

16.12–13  I . . . men · 73.5 [III.i.42].

16.13–14  hold me pace · 73.11 [III.i.48].

16.14–15  gelding . . . continent · 75.17 [III.i.109].

16.15–17  honey . . . much · 86.8–10 [III.ii.71–3]; line in margin (erased); 'sweetness . . . much' underlined (erased).

16.17     aweary · 86.25 [III.ii.88].

16.18 Sc · Scott. The references below are to *The Lay of the Last Minstrel*, in *Poetical Works* (see 4.1 n.).

16.18     seems as · VI.ii.10 (39).

16.18     at this tide · VI.iv.1 (39).

16.19     the rites of spousal · VI.iv.2 (39): 'the spousal rite'. Also VI.vi.1 (40): 'The spousal rites'.

16.19     benison · VI.vi.14 (40).

16.19     port · VI.xiii.2 (42).

17.1      Orcades · VI.xxi.10 (44).

17.2 She · Shelley. The references below are to *The Revolt of Islam*, in *Queen Mab, and Other Poems* (see 11.12 n.).

17.2      that ill . . . him · V.xxx.3 (149).

17.3      the day whereon · V.xxxvii.1–2 (151): 'that great day | Whereon'; cf. 12.2.

17.4      an aerial hymn · V.xli.9 (153).

17.4      disk . . . earth · V.l.1–2 (155).

17.5      blinding . . . morning · V[Laone's song].i.3 (156).

17.6 Col · Coleridge. The references below are to line and (in parentheses) page number of *The Poems of Samuel Taylor Coleridge*, ed. Derwent and Sara Coleridge (London: Edward Moxon, 1859). TH's copy (DCM) has his ink signature, dated 1865, on the front endpaper and contains a few pencil markings.

17.6     the gentle dew-fall · 'Fears in Solitude', 203 (173); cf. 63.11.

17.6–7     terms . . . tongues · 'Fears in Solitude', 114 (170).

17.7     aslant · 'Fears in Solitude', 207 (173).

17.8     a three years child · *The Rime of the Ancient Mariner*, 15 (93).

17.8     may'st · *Ancient Mariner*, 8 (93).

17.9 She · Shelley. The references below are to *The Revolt of Islam*, in *Queen Mab, and Other Poems* (see 11.12 n.).

17.9     ken · V[Laone's song].iii.13 (157).

17.9     shall cull from thought · V[Laone's song].v.12 (158): 'from thought all glorious forms shall cull'.

17.9–10     mists . . . woof · V.lii.1–2 (158).

17.10     moveless · V.liii.7 (159).

17.11     infinite throng · V.lii.2 (158).

17.11     speechless · V.liii.9 (159).

17.12–13     Earth . . . Autumn · V.lv.1, 3 (159): 'Earth, the general mother, | Pours from her fairest bosom, when. . .'.

17.13     every look . . . form · V.lvii.2–3 (160): 'every deepest look and holiest mind | Fed . . .'.

17.14     the dusky main · V.lvii.9 (160); cf. 15.5.

17.14–15     weaving . . . themes · VI.i.2 (161).

17.16     by the . . . driven · VI.ii.6–7 (161).

17.17     artillery's bolt · VI.iv.9 (162).

17.17–18     the dead & the alive · VI.vi.7 (162).

17.18     term · VI.xviii.3 (166).

17.19     I heard . . . pants · VI.xx.6–7 (166): 'I saw the shape its might which swayed, | And heard . . .'.

18.1     with mountain . . . dispread · VI.xxvi.9 (168); cf. 4.13.

18.1–2     the baffled heart · VI.xxxi.2 (169); line in margin.

18.2     blasts · VI.xxxii.7 (170); underlined and line in margin. Cf. 11.12.

18.2–3     strewed . . . sounds · VI.xxxii.8 (170); line in margin.

18.3–4     the sickness . . . joy · VI.xxxiv.6–7 (170).

18.4     the thick . . . hair · VI.xxxiii.2–3 (170); line in margin.

18.5     gentle might · VI.xxxix.7 (172).

18.5–6     those who . . . love · VI.xl.1–2 (172).

18.6–7     our talk . . . ruin · VI.xlii.4–5 (172–3).

18.7     wh made its floor · VI.li.5 (175).

18.8 By · Byron. The references below are to *Childe Harold's Pilgrimage*, in *Poems* (see 4.3 n.).

18.8            laying . . . prone · III.cvi.8 (580).

18.8–9          rear their leaves · Perhaps suggested by III.civ.9 (579): 'the Alps have rear'd a throne', and III.ci.8 (579): 'light leaves'.

18.9            hiving wisdom · III.cvii.2 (580).

18.10           irony, that master-spell · III.cvii.6 (580).

18.10           compels · III.cix.9 (580).

18.11 Sha · Shakespeare. The references below are to *Dramatic Works*; those in square brackets are to *The Riverside Shakespeare* (see 3.4 n.).

18.11           doff · *1 Henry IV*, V.114.7 [V.i.12].

18.11–12        unknit . . . war · *1 Henry IV*, V.114.10–11 [V.i.15–16].

18.12–13        move . . . again · *1 Henry IV*, V.114.12 [V.i.17]; cf. 10.11.

18.13           a portent · *1 Henry IV*, V.114.15 [V.i.20].

18.14           broached · *1 Henry IV*, V.114.16 [V.i.21].

18.14           unborn time · *1 Henry IV*, V.114.16 [V.i.21]: 'unborn times'.

18.15           outdare · *1 Henry IV*, V.115.12 [V.i.40].

18.15           sufferances borne · *1 Henry IV*, V.115.23 [V.i.51]: 'sufferances that you had borne'.

18.15           to forge · *1 Henry IV*, V.116.13 [V.i.68]: 'have forg'd'.

18.16           impaint · *1 Henry IV*, V.117.2 [V.i.80].

18.16–17        trimmed . . . tongue · *1 Henry IV*, V.121.6 [V.ii.56].

18.17–18        vaunting enemies · *1 Henry IV*, V.125.2 [V.iii.42].

18.18–19        ill . . . shrunk · *1 Henry IV*, V.129.14 [V.iv.88].

18.19–19.1      from . . . west · *2 Henry IV*, V.159.3 [Ind.3]; 'drooping' underlined.

19.1            apter · *2 Henry IV*, V.164.18 [I.i.69]; line in margin (erased); cf. 21.1.

19.2–3          the ragged'st . . . bring · *2 Henry IV*, V.167.19 [I.i.151]; footnoted.

19.3            lean · *2 Henry IV*, V.168.8 [I.i.164]; cf. 20.13.

19.3            presurmise · *2 Henry IV*, V.168.12 [I.i.168].

19.3–5          as . . . bachelor · *2 Henry IV*, V.172.4–5 [I.ii.26–7].

19.6 By · Byron. The references below are to *Childe Harold's Pilgrimage*, in *Poems* (see 4.3 n.).

19.6            a harmless wile · III.cxii.2 (581); cf. 38.3.

19.6            to fleet along · III.cxii.3 (581): 'fleet along'; cf. 46.4.

19.7            loss or guerdon · III.cxii.8 (581).

19.7–8          I have . . . breath · III.cxiii.2 (581).

19.8–9          bowed . . . knee · III.cxiii.2–3 (581): 'bow'd | To its idolatries a patient knee'.

19.9          coined . . . smiles · III.cxiii.4 (581).

19.10         respire · III.cxviii.7 (582).

19.10         is skilful to diffuse · IV.vi.9 (586); double line in margin.

19.11         over-weening phantasies · IV.vii.8 (586).

19.12–13      I've . . . tongues · IV.viii.1 (586).

19.13–14      and light . . . head · IV.x.3 (587).

19.15 Mi · Milton. The references below are to line and (in parentheses) page number of Book I of *Paradise Lost*, in *The Poetical Works of John Milton* (Halifax: Milner & Sowerby, 1865). TH's copy (DCM) has his signature in pencil, dated 1866, on the half-title and a second signature and '16 Westbourne Park Villas' in ink over pencil on the title-page. The volume is heavily marked and contains some annotation. Although TH's copy (DCM) of *The Poetical Works of John Milton* (London: Routledge, Warne, & Routledge, 1864), signed 'T. Hardy. 1865.', also contains numerous markings and a few annotations, the underlining in the Milner & Sowerby volume of many of the words quoted in the notebook suggests that it was TH's source.

19.15         tree . . . taste · 2 (1); 'whose mortal taste' underlined (erased).

19.15–16      secret top · 6 (2); underlined (erased).

19.16         the deep . . . Hell · 28 (2).

19.16–17      seduced . . . revolt · 33 (2).

19.17         baleful eyes · 56 (3); underlined (erased).

19.18         utmost pole · 74 (3); underlined (erased). Cf. 16.2.

19.18         sights of woe · 64 (3); 'sights' underlined (erased).

19.19         urges · 68 (3); underlined (erased).

19.19         the potent victor · 95 (4).

20.1          can else inflict · 96 (4).

20.1          outward lustre · 97 (4).

20.2 Swin · Algernon Charles Swinburne. The references below are to page and line number of *Chastelard: A Tragedy* (London: Edward Moxon, 1865). Also supplied, in square brackets, are page and line numbers of the Bonchurch Edition, *The Complete Works of Algernon Charles Swinburne*, ed. Edmund Gosse and Thomas James Wise, vol. VIII (London: William Heinemann, 1926). DCM has a copy of *Chastelard* with TH's pencil signature on the title-page written over an erased ink signature of the previous owner, H. L. MacKay, but since this is a US edition (New York: Hurd and Houghton, 1866) it is unlikely to have been in TH's hands by 1866 itself. There are no markings in the volume.

20.2–3        for all . . . days · 200.6 [122.3].

20.3          all will . . . you · 201.6 [122.20].

20.3–4        the dull . . . me · 154.8–9 [95.6–7].

20.4          sharp joy · 38.11 [27.19].

20.5–6        some . . . mouth · 38.16–39.1 [27.24–5].

| | |
|---|---|
| 20.7 | bound . . . flesh · 68.6 [44.3]. |
| 20.7 | at naked ebb · 38.16 [27.24]. |
| 20.8 | dead lute strain · 38.14 [27.22]; cf. 3.18, 28.17. |
| 20.8 | have . . . us · 68.10 [44.7]; cf. 43.7–8. |
| 20.8–9 | shut . . . it · 39.5 [28.2]. |
| 20.9 | the least . . . back · 68.8 [44.5]. |
| 20.10 | the great . . . joined · 69.3 [44.15]. |
| 20.10–11 | I c$^d$ . . . some · 69.10–11 [44.22–3]. |
| 20.11–12 | my heart . . . thirst · 69.19 [44.31]. |

20.13 Sha · Shakespeare. The references below are to *Henry IV. Part II*, in vol. V of *Dramatic Works*; those in square brackets are to *The Riverside Shakespeare* (see 3.4 n.).

| | |
|---|---|
| 20.13 | lean on your health · 168.8 [I.i.164]; cf. 19.3. |
| 20.14–15 | would . . . ranged · 169.2 [I.i.174]; cf. 10.5. |
| 20.15 | this stiff-borne action · 169.5 [I.i.177]: 'The stiff-borne action'. |
| 20.15–16 | brought forth · 169.6 [I.i.178]. |
| 20.16–17 | the gain . . . feared · 169.11–12 [I.i.183–4]. |
| 20.17–18 | wrought out life · 169.10 [I.i.182]. |
| 20.18 | up · 169.17 [I.i.189]. |
| 20.19 | this . . . mind · 170.9 [I.i.211]. |
| 21.1 | the aptest way · 170.11 [I.i.213]; cf. 19.1. |
| 21.1 | counter · 174.18 [I.ii.90]: 'hunt-counter'; footnoted. |
| 21.1–2 | all . . . home · 178.26–7 [I.ii.207–8]; 'kiss my lady peace' under-lined. |
| 21.2–3 | baying . . . heels · 183.23 [I.iii.80]. |
| 21.3–6 | but . . . life · 239.15–18 [IV.i.63–6]; cf. 41.9. |
| 21.6–7 | torrent of occasion · 239.24 [IV.i.72]. |
| 21.7–8 | the summary . . . griefs · 239.25 [IV.i.73]. |
| 21.8 | any branch of it · 240.10 [IV.i.85]. |
| 21.8 | newly · 240.5 [IV.i.80]; cf. 75.18. |
| 21.9 | concurring · 240.12 [IV.i.87]. |
| 21.9 | to seal · 240.16 [IV.i.91]: 'should seal'. |
| 21.9–10 | the edge of · 240.18 [absent from *Riverside Shakespeare*]: 'commotion's bitter edge' (although TH's source was probably the explanatory footnote, '*Commotion's bitter edge?* that is, *the edge of bitter strife and commotion*'). |
| 21.10 | bruises · 241.4 [IV.i.98]. |

21.11 Word · Wordsworth. The references below are to 'Descriptive Sketches', in *Poetical Works* (see 3.14 n.).

| | |
|---|---|
| 21.11 | Sad vacuities · 1 (30). |
| 21.11 | bourn · 6 (30). |

21.12      crazing care · 27 (30).

21.12      nod · 35 (30).

21.12      swelling · 47 (31); cf. 30.2.

21.13      thrown between · 53 (31).

21.13      upstayed · 118 (32).

21.14      mists . . . gale · 131 (32).

21.14      moveless · 132 (32).

21.15      the beams . . . between · 133 (32).

21.16      lengthens · 136 (32).

21.16      dewy lights · 138 (32).

21.17      dilated · 144 (32).

21.18 By · Byron. The references below are to *Childe Harold's Pilgrimage*, in *Poems* (see 4.3 n.).

21.18      and on . . . pausing · IV.lxxv.3 (600).

21.19      infant · IV.lxxiii.2 (600).

21.19      gird · IV.lxix.9 (599); cf. 59.11.

21.19      to understand, not feel · IV.lxxvii.3 (600).

22.1       thy lyric flow · IV.lxxvii.3 (600).

22.2 Recoll · Recollections, i.e. words and phrases recalled either from TH's reading or conversation (cf. 'Var$^s$' at 8.1 and n.). He was perhaps familiar with John William Burgon's 'Petra' ('A rose-red city "half as old as time"') and he could have found 'looby' in Boswell's *Life of Johnson* (see 77.9 n.) or Disraeli's *Sybil*, but many of the other words are dialect forms: *OED*, for example, cites TH's own novels among its examples of 'nammet' (a variant spelling of 'nammut') and as its only examples of 'dand'.

22.10 Burns · Robert Burns. The references below are to stanza, line, and (in parentheses) page number of *The Poetical Works of Robert Burns*, ed. Robert Aris Willmott (London: Routledge, Warne, & Routledge, 1863). TH's copy (Beinecke) contains no signature, but it does contain a few markings including an addition to the contents page.

22.10      flaunting · 'To a Mountain Daisy', iv.1 (107).

22.10      sunward · 'To a Mountain Daisy', v.2 (107).

22.11      nature sickened · 'The Braes o' Ballochmyle', i.4 (293).

22.11      silk-saft · 'O were my love yon lilac fair', iv.3 (326).

22.12 Gol T · *The Golden Treasury*. The references below are to *The Golden Treasury* (see 8.8 n.).

22.12      that wave . . . to · Anon. [George Darley], 'The Loveliness of Love' ['A Song': 'It is not beauty I demand'], v.2 (73).

22.13      To cease . . . midnight · John Keats, 'Ode to a Nightingale', vi.6 (245); 'upon' underlined (erased).

22.14 Inv · Inventions (i.e. TH's own experimentations); cf. 32.16.

22.16 Shak · Shakespeare. The references below are to *Hamlet*, in vol. IX of *Dramatic Works*; those in square brackets are to *The Riverside Shakespeare* (see 3.4 n.).

22.16          niggard of question · 218.17 [III.i.13].

22.16          edge · 219.13 [III.i.26].

22.17          colour · 220.6 [III.i.44].

22.17          smart lash · 220.11 [III.i.49]: 'How smart a lash'.

22.18          shock · 221.3 [III.i.61]: 'shocks'.

22.18          awry · 223.4 [III.i.86].

22.18          as lief · 227.13 [III.ii.3].

22.18          cope with · 230.12 [III.ii.55]: 'cop'd withal'; cf. 46.1.

23.1           loth · 235, stage direction for dumb show [*Riverside Shakespeare* reads 'harsh']; cf. 4.12.

23.1           mich · 235.2 [III.ii.137]: 'miching'; against the footnote definition, 'To *mich*, for to *skulk*, to *lurk*, was an old English verb in common use in Shakespeare's time', TH drew a line and wrote 'still in use in Dorset'.

23.1           tax him home · 248.3 [III.iii.29].

23.2           bound to · 248.15 [III.iii.41]; 'to double business bound'.

23.3           to buy out · 249.8 [III.iii.60]: 'Buys out'.

23.4           bow · 249.18 [III.iii.70].

23.4           wring your heart · 253.6 [III.iv.35].

23.5 Isa · Isaiah. The references below are to chapter and verse of the Book of Isaiah, in the Authorized Version of the Bible. The front flyleaf of TH's Bible (DCM) is inscribed in ink over pencil 'Tho⁵ Hardy. 1861.' and in pencil only '1862—Clarence Place—Kilburn.' The volume contains some markings, especially in the Book of Job, and numerous dates.

23.5           Thy . . . loosed · xxxiii.23.

23.5–6         works . . . delight · Evidently a TH invention (note the absence of quotation marks), perhaps suggested by xix.9: 'work in fine flax'; cf. Psalm lviii.2: 'ye work wickedness'.

23.6           trodden down · lxiii.18.

23.7           that fly as a cloud · lx.8.

23.8 By · Byron. The references below are to *Childe Harold's Pilgrimage*, in *Poems* (see 4.3 n.).

23.8           the waves . . me · III.ii.2 (556); cf. 28.11.

23.8–9         strew the gale · III.ii.6 (556); cf. 28.13–14.

23.9           Still . . . on · III.ii.7 (556); cf. 28.14.

23.9–10        again . . . theme · III.iii.3 (556); cf. 28.14.

23.10          the last . . . life · III.iii.9 (556).

23.11          so it . . . it · III.iv.6 (556): 'So that it'; cf. 28.18.

23.11          nor . . . love · III.v.3–4 (556).

23.12     he drooped · III.xv.1, 3 (558): 'he . . . Droop'd'.

23.13     woos us · III.xiv.9 (558).

23.13     where rose the mount$^s$ · III.xiii.1 (558).

23.14     tire of · III.xlii.7–8 (564); cf. 31.12.

23.14     chiefless castles · III.xlvi.8 (565).

23.15 Mem · Memorandum. 'comp & sup.' = comparative and superlative.

23.17 Shak · Shakespeare. The references below are to *The Two Gentlemen of Verona*, in vol. I of *Dramatic Works*; those in square brackets are to *The Riverside Shakespeare* (see 3.4 n.).

23.17     say No · 117.15 [I.ii.55].

23.17     cast my love · 116.9 [I.ii.25].

24.1      I chid hence · 117.20 [I.ii.60]: 'I chid Lucetta hence'.

24.3      to relish a love song · 125.2 [II.i.20].

24.3–4    I . . . movingly · 128.23 [II.i.128].

24.4–5    And Silvia . . . Ethiope · 143.15–16 [II.vi.25–6]: 'And Silvia, (witness heaven, that made her fair!) | Shews . . .'.

24.6      aiming at · 143.20 [II.vi.30].

24.7      as far from fraud · 146.25 [II.vii.78].

24.7–8    a hard opinion · 147.2 [II.vii.81].

24.9 Bur · Burns. The references below are to 'The Vision', in *Poetical Works* (see 22.10 n.).

24.9      scrimply · I.xi.2 (53); footnoted.

24.9–10   the sun . . . day · I.i.1 (51).

24.10     peer it · I.xi.4 (53).

24.11     drew . . . wonder · I.xii.2 (53): 'My gazing wonder chiefly drew'.

24.12–13  and hermit . . . woods · I.xiv.3 (53): 'Auld hermit Ayr staw thro' his woods'; footnoted and line in margin.

24.16 Wor · Wordsworth. The references below are to 'Lines, Composed a Few Miles Above Tintern Abbey', in *Poetical Works* (see 3.14 n.).

24.16     wreaths . . . up · 18–19 (159).

24.16–17  affect$^{ns}$ . . . on · 43 (160).

25.1 In Mem · *In Memoriam*. The references below are to the first edition (London: Edward Moxon, 1850). If TH owned copies of Tennyson at this early period they seem not to have survived. Because the wording of two of TH's quotations conforms to that of the pre-1851 editions and because there is no reference to the section beginning 'O Sorrow, wilt thou live with me' (LIX in Tennyson's final version but first added, as LVIII, to the fourth edition of 1851), the first edition has been taken as the primary reference text, with supplementary references in square brackets to the final numbering of the sections as given in *The Poems of Tennyson*, ed. Christopher Ricks, 2nd edn., 3 vols. (Harlow: Longman, 1987), II.304–459. TH's '70' after the abbreviated title refers to the page on which XLVII appears.

| | |
|---|---|
| 25.1 | closed grave doubts · XLVII.i.2–3 (70) [XLVIII]. |
| 25.2 | ~~these grave~~ · Evidently the beginning of an abandoned variation; see preceding entry. |
| 25.2 | slender . . . doubt · XLVII.ii.3 (70) [XLVIII]. |
| 25.3 | vassal unto love · XLVII.ii.4 (70) [XLVIII]. |
| 25.3 | loosens from · XLVII.iv.2 (70) [XLVIII]. |
| 25.4 | the schools · XLVIII.i.1 (71) [XLIX]. |
| 25.4 | glance from · XLVIII.i.1–2 (71) [XLIX]: 'From art, from nature, from the schools, \| Let random influences glance'. |
| 25.5 | breaks . . . pools · XLVIII.i.4 (71) [XLIX]. |
| 25.5–6 | the fancy's . . . eddy · XLVIII.ii.2 (71) [XLIX]. |
| 25.6 | be with . . . low · XLIX.i.1 (72) [L]: 'Be near me . . .'. |
| 25.7 | when my . . . dry · XLIX.iii.1 (72) [L]. |
| 25.7 | to point · XLIX.iv.2 (72) [L]. |
| 25.8 | vileness · L.i.4 (73) [LI]. |
| 25.8–9 | and I . . . love · L.ii.4 (73) [LI]; cf. 16.9. |
| 25.9 | love . . . beloved · LI.i.2 (74) [LII]. |
| 25.10 | topmost froth · LI.i.4 (74) [LII]; cf. 11.14. |
| 25.10 | dash'd with · LI.iv.2 (74) [LII]. |
| 25.11 | sunder'd · LI.iv.4 (74) [LII]. |
| 25.11 | heats of youth · LII.iii.2 (75) [LIII]; cf. 71.12. |
| 25.11 | preach · LII.iii.3 (75) [LIII]. |
| 25.12 | slope . . . God · LIV.iv.4 (78) [LV]. |
| 25.13 | lame hands · LIV.v.1 (79) [LV]. |
| 25.13 | scarped cliff · LV.i.2 (80) [LVI]. |
| 25.13–14 | roll'd the psalm · LV.iii.3 (80) [LVI]. |
| 25.14 | crypt · LVII.ii.4 (83) [LVIII]: 'crypts', |
| 25.14–15 | she sighs . . . days · LVIII.iii.2 (84) [LX]. |
| 25.15 | tease her · LVIII.iv.2 (84) [LX]. |
| 25.15–16 | change replies · LIX.i.2 (85) [LXI]. |
| 25.16 | the circle of the wise · LIX.i.3 (85) [LXI]. |
| 25.17 | vaster · LXI.iii.2 (87) [LXIII]. |
| 25.17 | a higher . . . deep · LXI.iii.4 (87) [LXIII]. |
| 25.18 | to round · LXI.iii.3 (87) [LXIII]: 'round'. |
| 25.18–19 | divinely gifted man · LXII.i.2 (88) [LXIV]. |
| 25.19 | invidious bar · LXII.ii.1 (88) [LXIV]. |
| 25.19–26.3 | the skirts . . . star · LXII.ii.2–4 (88) [LXIV]. |
| 26.3 | to mould · LXII.iii.3 (88) [LXIV]; cf. 11.6. |
| 26.3–4 | and shape . . . throne · LXII.iii.4 (88) [LXIV]. |
| 26.4–5 | crowning slope · LXII.iv.2 (88) [LXIV]. |

| | |
|---|---|
| 26.5–6 | a distant . . . stream · LXII.v.3–4 (89) [LXIV]. |
| 26.7 | his narrower fate · LXII.vi.1 (89) [LXIV]. |
| 26.7–8 | I lull . . . trouble-tost · LXIII.i.2 (90) [LXV]. |
| 26.8 | move . . . to · LXIII.iii.4 (90) [LXV]. |
| 26.9 | till . . . gray · LXV.iii.4 (92) [LXVII]. |
| 26.9–10 | times my breath · LXVI.i.2 (93) [LXVIII]. |
| 26.10 | knows not · LXVI.i.3 (93) [LXVIII]. |
| 26.11 | resolve the doubt · LXVI.iii.4 (93) [LXVIII]. |
| 26.11 | reached · LXVII.v.1 (95) [LXIX]. |
| 26.12 | touch . . . leaf · LXVII.v.2 (95) [LXIX]. |
| 26.12 | wizard music roll · LXVIII.iv.2 (96) [LXX]. |
| 26.13 | dark bulks · LXVIII.iii.3 (96) [LXX]. |
| 26.13–14 | a night-long . . . Past · LXIX.i.3 (97) [LXXI]. |
| 26.14 | treble strong · LXIX.ii.2 (97) [LXXI: 'trebly strong']. |
| 26.14–15 | grow to · LXIX.iii.3 (97) [LXXI]. |
| 26.15 | the river's reach · LXIX.iv.1 (97) [LXXI]: 'the river's wooded reach'. |
| 26.15–16 | the cataract . . . bridge · LXIX.iv.3 (97) [LXXI]. |
| 26.16–17 | Day . . . flame · LXX.ii.1, iv.1 (98) [LXXII]: 'Day . . . \| Who might'st . . .'; cf. 33.6. |
| 26.18 | beam & shade · LXX.iv.3 (98) [LXXII]. |
| 26.18 | chequerwork · LXX.iv.3 (98) [LXXII]. |
| 26.18 | lift · LXX.vi.1 (99) [LXXII]. |
| 26.19 | sow . . . boughs · LXX.vi.4 (99) [LXXII]. |
| 26.19–27.1 | thick noon · LXX.vii.2 (99) [LXXII]. |
| 27.1 | joyless gray · LXX.vii.3 (99) [LXXII]. |
| 27.1 | kindred with · LXXII.ii.4 (101) [LXXIV]. |
| 27.3–4 | The world . . . been · LXXIII.iv.3–4 (102) [LXXV]. |
| 27.5 | set . . . where · LXXIV.i.2–3 (104) [LXXVI]. |
| 27.5–6 | take . . . foresight · LXXIV.ii.1 (104) [LXXVI]. |
| 27.6 | ring with · LXXV.iv.2 (105) [LXXVII]. |
| 27.6–7 | snow . . . earth · LXXVI.i.3 (106) [LXXVIII]. |
| 27.7–8 | no . . . slept · LXXVI.ii.2 (106) [LXXVIII]. |
| 27.9 | the winters left behind · LXXVI.iii.1 (106) [LXXVIII]. |
| 27.10 | O last . . . die · LXXVI.v.1 (107) [LXXVIII]. |
| 27.11 | mixt with · LXXVI.v.2 (107) [LXXVIII]; cf. 29.4, 33.12. |
| 27.11 | dropt on · LXXVIII.i.4 (110) [LXXX]: 'dropt the dust on'. |
| 27.12 | then . . . can · LXXVIII.ii.1 (110) [LXXX]. |
| 27.13 | unused . . . grave · LXXVIII.iv.3 (110) [LXXX]. |
| 27.13 | feud · LXXX.i.1 (112) [LXXXII]. |

| | |
|---|---|
| 27.14–15 | transplanted . . . otherwhere · LXXX.iii.3 (112) [LXXXII]. |
| 27.15 | garners in · LXXX.iv.2 (112) [LXXXII]. |
| 27.16 | dip down upon · LXXXI.i.1 (113) [LXXXIII]. |
| 27.16–17 | stays thee from · LXXXI.ii.1 (113) [LXXXIII]. |
| 27.17 | to meet . . . desire · LXXXII.v.1 (115) [LXXXIV]. |
| 27.18 | lavish · LXXXII.ix.2 (115) [LXXXIV]. |
| 27.18 | gave him welcome · LXXXIII.vi.4 (118) [LXXXV]. |
| 27.18 | poised · LXXXIII.ix.1 (118) [LXXXV]: 'equal-poised'. |
| 27.19 | I count it crime · LXXXIII.xvi.1 (120) [LXXXV]. |
| 27.19–28.1 | my old . . . tomb · LXXXIII.xix.3 (120) [LXXXV]. |
| 28.1 | stain · LXXXIII.xxii.1 (121) [LXXXV]. |
| 28.1 | gorgeous · LXXXIV.i.2 (124) [LXXXVI]. |
| 28.2 | the round of space · LXXXIV.ii.1 (124) [LXXXVI]. |
| 28.2 | gray flats · LXXXV.iv.1 (125) [LXXXVII]. |
| 28.3 | aim fair · LXXXV.vii.1 (126) [LXXXVII]: 'aim an arrow fair'. |
| 28.3 | fierce extremes · LXXXVI.ii.1 (128) [LXXXVIII]. |
| 28.3 | dusking · LXXXVI.ii.2 (128) [LXXXVIII: 'darkening']. |
| 28.4 | midmost · LXXXVI.ii.3 (128) [LXXXVIII]; cf. 49.8. |
| 28.4 | counterchange · LXXXVII.i.1 (129) [LXXXIX]. |
| 28.4 | towering · LXXXVII.i.4 (129) [LXXXIX]. |
| 28.5 | to rout . . . cares · LXXXVII.v.1 (130) [LXXXIX]. |
| 28.5 | whereat · LXXXVII.ix.1 (130) [LXXXIX]. |
| 28.6 | the books . . . hate · LXXXVII.ix.2 (130) [LXXXIX]. |
| 28.7 | couch'd · LXXXVII.xi.4 (131) [LXXXIX]. |
| 28.7–8 | to talk them o'er · LXXXVIII.iii.3 (132) [XC]. '(133)' = TH's memorandum of the page (containing the conclusion of LXXXVIII) at which he broke off. |

28.9 By. Ch H. C III. · Byron, *Childe Harold's Pilgrimage*, Canto III. The references below are to *Childe Harold's Pilgrimage*, in *Poems* (see 4.3 n.).

| | |
|---|---|
| 28.9 | sole daughter · III.i.2 (555). |
| 28.9–10 | the waters heave · III.i.6 (555). |
| 28.10 | the winds . . . voices · III.i.7 (555). |
| 28.10 | whither · III.i.8 (555). |
| 28.11 | glad mine eye · III.i.9 (555). |
| 28.11 | the waves bound · III.ii.2 (556); cf. 23.8. |
| 28.11–12 | a steed . . . rider · III.ii.2–3 (556). |
| 28.12 | guidance · III.ii.4 (556). |
| 28.12–13 | strained mast · III.ii.5 (556). |
| 28.13 | to quiver · III.ii.5 (556): 'should quiver'. |
| 28.13 | rent canvass · III.ii.6 (556). |

28.13–14    strew the gale · III.ii.6 (556); cf. 23.8–9.

28.14       still must I on · III.ii.7 (556); cf. 23.9.

28.14–15    I seize . . . me · III.iii.3 (556): '. . . theme, then but begun, | And
            . . .'; cf. 23.9–10.

28.15–16    the journeying years · III.iii.8 (556).

28.16       harp . . . string · III.iv.2 (556).

28.16–17    heart . . . jar · III.iv.2–3 (556).

28.17       as I . . . sing · III.iv.4 (556).

28.17       strain · III.iv.5 (556); cf. 3.18, 20.8.

28.18       wean me from · III.iv.6 (556).

28.18–19    so it . . . me · III.iv.7–8 (556); cf. 23.11.

28.19       piercing . . . life · III.v.2 (556).

29.1        so that . . . waits him · III.v.3 (556).

29.1–2      cut to his heart · III.v.5 (556).

29.2        endurance · III.v.6 (556).

29.2–3      why . . . caves · III.v.7 (556).

29.3        rife . . . images · III.v.7–8 (556).

29.4        live . . . intense · III.vi.1–2 (556).

29.4–5      mix'd . . . spirit · III.vi.8 (556); cf. 27.11, 33.12.

29.5        thy birth · III.vi.8 (556).

29.5–6      feeling with thee · III.vi.9 (556): 'feeling still with thee'.

29.6        to think wildly · III.vii.1 (557): 'think less wildly'.

29.8        o'erwrought · III.vii.3 (557).

29.8        phantasy · III.vii.4 (557).

29.8–9      yet . . . same · III.vii.7 (557): 'Yet am I changed; though still
            enough the same'.

29.9        time cannot abate · III.vii.8 (557).

29.10       fain · III.viii.4 (557); cf. 15.15, 49.13.

29.10       he of the breast · III.viii.4 (557).

29.10       wrung with · III.viii.5 (557).

29.11       years . . . mind · III.viii.7–8 (557).

29.12 Sha · Shakespeare. The references below are to *Richard II*, in vol. IV
of *Dramatic Works*; those in square brackets are to *The Riverside Shakespeare* (see
3.4 n.).

29.12       to make good · 405.13 [I.i.37]: 'shall make good'.

29.12–13    our . . . hear · 404.3 [I.i.5].

29.13–14    moreover . . . him · 404.6 [I.i.8]: 'moreover, hast thou . . .'.

29.14–15    on some . . . of · 404.9 [I.i.11].

29.15       sift him · 404.10 [I.i.12].

29.15       seen in · 404.11 [I.i.13].

29.16    frowning brow to brow · 404.14 [I.i.16]; in TH's note the short-hand = 'therefore loving lip to lip'.

29.17    freely · 404.15 [I.i.17].

29.17    add to · 404.22 [I.i.24]: 'Add an immortal title to'.

29.17    tendering · 405.8 [I.i.32].

29.17    hush'd · 405.29 [I.i.53].

29.18    to spur · 405.31 [I.i.55]: 'spurs'.

29.18    were . . . run · 406.8 [I.i.63].

29.18    rites · 406.20 [I.i.75].

29.19    how high a pitch · 408.1 [I.i.109].

29.19    bid be · 408.4 [I.i.112]: 'bid his ears a little while be'.

29.19    a trespass · 409.6 [I.i.138].

30.1     chambered with · 409.17 [I.i.149]: 'chamber'd in'.

30.1–2   where . . . harbour · 411.15 [I.i.195].

30.2–3   the swelling . . . hate · 411.21 [I.i.201]; cf. 21.12.

30.3     gage · 411.6 [I.i.186].

31.3–4   put . . . heaven · 412.8 [I.ii.6].

30.5     hack'd down · 412.22 [I.ii.20].

30.6 G.T. Mil · *Golden Treasury*, Milton. The references below are to 'Ode on the Morning of Christ's Nativity', in *The Golden Treasury* (see 8.8 n.).

30.6     afford . . . God · iii.2 (41).

30.7     work us · i.7 (41).

30.7–8   the heaven . . . light · iii.5–6 (41).

30.9     join to · iv.6 (42): 'join thy voice unto'.

30.9–10  if such . . . long · 'The Hymn', xiv.1–2 (45).

3.10     melt from · 'The Hymn', xiv.6 (45).

30.10–11 the tissued clouds · 'The Hymn', xv.6 (45).

30.11    casts . . . sway · 'The Hymn', xviii.6 (45).

30.12    a breathéd spell · 'The Hymn', xix.7 (46); in TH's note the short-hand = 'love'.

30.13    edged . . . pale · 'The Hymn', xx.5 (46).

30.13    dismal · 'The Hymn', xxiii.6 (47).

30.13    unshowered · 'The Hymn', xxiv.3 (47).

30.14    curtained . . . red · 'The Hymn', xxvi.2 (47)

30.14–15 the flocking . . . jail · 'The Hymn', xxvi.4–5 (47).

30.16    slips . . . grave · 'The Hymn', xxvi.6 (47); cf. 45.17.

30.16    maze · 'The Hymn', xxvi.8 (47).

30.17 Dry · John Dryden. The reference below is to 'Song for Saint Cecilia's Day', in *The Golden Treasury* (see 8.8 n.).

30.17–18 notes . . . above · vi.5–6 (49).

30.19 Mil · Milton. The reference below is to 'On the Late Massacre in Piemont', in *The Golden Treasury* (see 8.8 n.).

30.19–31.1   their moans . . . heaven · 8–10 (50).

31.2 Marv · Andrew Marvell · The references below are to 'Horatian Ode upon Cromwell's Return from Ireland', in *The Golden Treasury* (see 8.8 n.).

31.2          where it was nurst · iv.2 (50).

31.2–3        the emulous, or enemy · v.2 (50).

31.3          his highest plot · viii.3 (51).

31.3–4        plead . . . vain · x.2 (51).

31.4          comely · xvi.3 (52); cf. 37.1.

31.4–5        the Public's skirt · xxiii.2 (52).

31.5          parti-coloured · xxvii.2 (53); in TH's note the shorthand = 'loved'.

31.5–6        victory . . . plume · xxv.2 (53).

31.7 Sha Rch^d II · Shakespeare, *Richard II*. The references below are to *Richard II*, in vol. IV of *Dramatic Works*; those in square brackets are to *The Riverside Shakespeare* (see 3.4 n.).

31.7          smooth his fault · 424.24 [I.iii.240]; line in margin (erased).

31.7–8        wake his peace · 420.14 [I.iii.132]: 'wake our peace'.

31.8          a foil · 425.20 [I.iii.266].

31.8          craft · 428.11 [I.iv.13]; recurs, underlined, at 429.2 [I.iv.28].

31.8–9        dive . . . hearts · 428.23 [I.iv.25].

31.9          throw away on · 429.1 [I.iv.27].

31.9          to farm · 429.19 [I.iv.45].

31.9–10       to make for · 429.26 [I.iv.52]: 'will make for'; in TH's note the shorthand = 'therefore loving'.

31.10         come short · 429.21 [I.iv.47].

31.10         to strive with · 430.14 [II.i.3]: 'strive not with'.

31.11         deep harmony · 430.17 [II.i.6].

31.11         spent, upon · 430.18 [II.i.7]: 'spent in vain'.

31.11         limp after · 431.15 [II.i.23]: 'Limps after'.

31.12         doth . . . vanity · 431.16 [II.i.24].

31.12         to tire · 432.5 [II.i.36]: 'tires'; cf. 23.14.

31.13         to rein · 433.12 [II.i.70]: 'being rein'd' [*Riverside Shakespeare* reads 'being rag'd'].

31.13         gaunt · 433.16 [II.i.74].

31.13–15      the pleasure . . . fast · 434.3–4 [II.i.79–80]; line in margin (erased). Cf. 74.1–2.

31.16 Exc. B.I. · 'The Excursion', Book I. The references below are to 'The Excursion', Book I, in *The Poetical Works of William Wordsworth* (see 3.14 n.).

31.16      showed . . . of · 4–5 (274): 'show'd far off | A surface dappled o'er with'.

31.16–17   careless limbs · 11 (274).

31.17      casts . . . own · 12–13 (274).

31.17      determined · 8 (274).

31.18      grateful resting pl · 20 (274): '. . . resting-place'.

31.18      livelier joy · 20 (274).

31.19      brotherhood · 29 (274).

31.19      slackened · 47 (275).

31.19      seated in a tract · 55 (275).

32.1       to wh he drew · 58 (275).

32.1       product · 71 (275).

32.1       dimmer · 162 (277).

32.2       plain presence · 80 (275).

32.2       feeling · 104 (276).

32.3       liver · 129 (275): 'livers'.

32.3       on his . . . lay · 154–5 (277).

32.4       braced · 330 (280).

32.4       equipoise · 384 (281).

32.4–5     a being . . . beings · 462–3 (283); line in margin.

32.5 By · Byron. The reference below is to *Childe Harold's Pilgrimage*, in *Poems* (see 4.3 n.).

32.5       sheathed · III.x.4 (557).

32.6 R^d II. Sha · *Richard II*, Shakespeare. The references below are to *Richard II*, in vol. IV of *Dramatic Works*; those in square brackets are to *The Riverside Shakespeare* (see 3.4 n.).

32.6       no whit lesser · 435.1 [II.i.103]; cf. 5.4, 59.10.

32.6       to sour · 437.13 [II.i.169]: 'made me sour'.

32.6       to prick to · 438.24 [II.i.207]: 'prick my tender patience to'.

32.7       seize . . . hands · 438.26 [II.i.209].

32.7–8     I'll . . . while · 438.28 [II.i.211].

32.8       fall out · 439.3 [II.i.214].

32.8–9     repair to · 439.5 [II.i.216].

32.9       break with · 439.17 [II.i.228].

32.9       the king is not himself · 440.1 [II.i.241].

32.10      to fine · 440.7 [II.i.247]: 'hath he fin'd'.

32.10      sit sore upon · 441.1 [II.i.265].

32.10      making hither · 442.7 [II.i.287].

32.10–11   to urge to · 442.19 [II.i.299]: 'urge doubts to'.

32.11      life-harming · 443.1 [II.ii.3]; in TH's note 'th^t ' = 'thought'.

| 32.12 | crave · 444.19 [II.ii.44]. |
|---|---|

32.12    broke his staff · 445.12 [II.ii.59]; in TH's note 'm.b.' = 'may/might be'.

32.13    prop · 446.14 [II.ii.82]: 'underprop'; line in margin (erased).

32.13    so . . . my · 447.3 [II.ii.101].

32.14    presages · 448.19 [II.ii.142].

32.14    draw out our miles · 449.5 [II.iii.5].

32.14    bereft · 439.26 [II.i.237].

32.15    I bethink me · 449.8 [II.iii.8].

32.16 Inv. · Inventions; cf. 22.14.

33.1 Sc. L. of I. · Scott, *The Lord of the Isles*. The references below are to *The Lord of the Isles*, in *Poetical Works* (see 4.1 n.).

33.1    his . . . on · I[Prologue].1–2 (411).

33.2    a shroud . . . gold · I[Prologue].3 (411).

33.3    Ettricke's western fell · I[Prologue].9 (411).

33.3    hushed · I[Prologue].15 (411).

33.4    forms of life · I[Prologue].16 (411).

33.4    Autumn's fading realms · I[Prologue].20 (411).

33.5    stain · I[Prologue].24 (411).

33.5    the waste fields · I[Prologue].25 (411); cf. 41.6.

33.5    to glean · I[Prologue].25 (411): 'the gleaner's way'. Also I[Prologue].34 (412): 'a lonely gleaner'. Cf. 8.6.

33.6    the Seer · I[Prologue].42 (412).

33.6    heaved . . . wave · I.i.4 (412); cf. 26.17.

33.7    symphony · I.i.11 (412).

33.7    festal day · I.i.16 (412); cf. 13.19.

33.7    descant · I.ii.2 (412).

33.7–8    high . . . ours · I.ii.3 (412).

33.8    to charm from · I.ii.4 (412): 'To charm dull sleep from'.

33.9    the summons of · I.ii.14 (412).

33.9–10    the eagle . . . cloud · I.ii.11–12 (412).

33.10–11    to mate . . . voice · I.iii.4 (412): 'To mate thy melody of voice'.

33.11    mocks · I.iii.6 (413).

33.12    mix . . . dream · I.iii.12 (413); cf. 27.11, 29.4–5.

33.12–14    wake . . . allow · I.iv.1–2 (413).

33.14–15    Fear . . . guest · I.iv.5 (413).

33.15    tamed . . . been · I.v.3 (413).

33.16    not . . . pride · I.v.5–6 (413).

33.17    their tenderest numbers · I.v.7 (413).

33.17–18    beauty's . . . power · I.vi.3 (413).

33.18      enhance · I.vi.6 (413): 'enhanced'.

33.18-19   for . . . lay · I.vi.12 (413).

33.19      a space apart · I.vii.7 (414).

34.1       cloistered · I.vii.14 (414).

34.1       her nursling · I.vii.15 (414): 'her nursling's'.

34.1-2     in finished loveliness · I.vii.19 (414).

34.2-4     where . . . shore · I.vii.23-4 (414).

34.4-5     each . . . reclined · I.viii.7 (414).

34.5       o'erawes · I.viii.10 (414).

34.6       engaging with · I.viii.12 (414): 'with his rocks engaging'.

34.6-7     given to fame · I.viii.22 (414).

34.7-8     flung . . . holy-tide · I.viii.35-6 (414).

34.8       her hurrying hand · I.ix.3 (414).

34.9       sum . . . lot · I.ix.17 (414).

34.10      the league . . . Edith · I.x.3-4 (415).

34.10-11   our . . . same · I.x.9 (415).

34.11-13   my . . . gale · I.x.10-12 (415).

34.13-14   void of energy · I.x.21 (415).

34.14      what requital · I.xi.3 (415).

34.14-15   some lighter love · I.xi.8 (415).

34.15      stoop her mast · I.xii.14 (415): 'Stoop to the freshening gale her mast'.

34.15-16   its bannered pride · I.xii.15 (415).

34.16-17   to win . . . gale · I.xiii.4 (415).

34.17      the scud comes on · I.xiii.7 (415): 'the darkening scud comes on'.

34.17-18   the rising wind · I.xiii.11 (415).

34.18      at every tack · I.xiii.14 (415).

34.18-19   they . . . seas · I.xv.1 (416).

34.19      the willing breeze · I.xv.2 (416).

34.19      swept by · I.xv.3 (416).

35.1       streamered . . . gold · I.xv.4 (416).

35.1-2     chafes beneath · I.xv.8 (416).

35.2       field-ward · I.xv.11 (416).

35.2-3     to the . . . minstrelsy · I.xv.19-20 (416); cf. 61.3-4.

35.3-4     come . . . Sound · I.xv.26 (416); cf. 5.6.

35.5       so bore they on · I.xvi.1 (416).

35.6 Sha: Rd II. · Shakespeare, *Richard II*. The references below are to *Richard II*, in vol. IV of *Dramatic Works*; those in square brackets are to *The Riverside Shakespeare* (see 3.4 n.).

35.6–7     learn . . . state · 463.2–3 [III.ii.116–17]: '. . . bows | Of double-
fatal yew against . . .'.

35.7       measure · 463.11 [III.ii.125]; for 'read', cf. 13.3, 14.16.

35.8       our confines · 463.11 [III.ii.125].

35.9 Dic,s · Dictionaries. TH's use of the plural suggests that he was drawing upon more than one source. Most of the words in this group, however,
occur in *The Standard Pronouncing Dictionary of the English Language*, ed. P. Austin
Nuttall (London: Routledge, Warne, & Routledge, 1864), of which TH's
copy (DCM) bears his signature opposite the title-page and the date 1865: his
definition of 'tucker' (35.14), for example, coincides almost word for word
with Nuttall's 'small piece of linen for shading the breast of women' (821).
Cf. 35.10 with 42.11.

36.1 Spen. Epith · Spenser, 'Epithalamion'. The references below are to
'Epithalamion', in *The Faerie Queene* (see 4.12 n.).

36.1       my truest turtle-dove · ii.6 (793).

36.2       crystal-bright · iv.9 (794).

36.2       ye lightfoot maids · iv.12 (794).

36.3       the birds' . . . song · v.15 (795).

36.4       dimmed by · vi.2–3 (795): 'dimmed were | With'; cf. 11.3.

36.4       daughters of delight · vi.5 (795).

36.7       to tower · iv.13 (794).

36.7–8     that do . . . allot · vi.9 (795): 'Which doe . . .'.

36.8–9     ye three . . . queen · vi.12 (795).

36.9       throw between · vi.15 (795).

36.10      in seemly good array · vii.5 (795).

36.10–11   sunshiny face · vii.10 (795).

36.11      sovereign praises · vii.18 (795).

36.11–12   the pipe . . . croud · viii.3 (795).

36.12–13   they their timbrels smite · viii.6 (796).

36.13      portly · ix.1 (796); line in margin.

36.13      do attire her · ix.9 (796): 'Doe lyke a golden mantle her attyre';
line in margin.

36.14      a garland green · ix.10 (796); line in margin.

36.14–15   modest eyes · ix.12 (796); line in margin.

36.15–16   adorned . . . store · x.4 (796); line in margin.

36.16      hath ruddied · x.7 (796); line in margin.

36.16      uncrudded · x.9 (796); line in margin.

36.17      her lively spright · xi.2 (797); line in margin. Cf. 37.3.

36.17–18   garnished . . . degree · xi.3 (797); line in margin.

36.18–19   there . . . chastity · xi.7 (797); line in margin. This line and the
following eight lines are also bracketed and annotated 'ELG' (i.e.

Emma Lavinia Gifford, whom TH met in 1870 and married in 1874).

37.1      unspottted . . . womanhood · xi.8 (797); line in margin. See also preceding note. Cf. 31.4.

37.2      chastity's sweet bower · x.14 (796); line in margin.

37.2      things uncomely · xi.14 (797); line in margin. See also 36.18–19 n.

37.3      as doth behove · xii.3 (797).

37.3      lively notes · xii.16 (797); cf. 36.17.

37.4      the red . . . cheeks · xiii.4 (797).

37.4–5    forget their service · xiii.9 (798).

37.5      eyes . . . on · xiii.12 (798).

37.5      a coronal · xiv.14 (798).

37.6      fitter · xv.12 (798).

37.6      slowly . . . spend · xvi.3 (799).

37.7      the Western foam · xvi.6 (799).

37.7      is nighing fast · xvii.3 (799).

37.7      plight · xxii.3 (801).

37.8      odoured · xvii.9 (799).

37.8      quietsome · xviii.12 (800).

37.8      young men · xviii.18 (800).

37.8      secret dark · xx.8 (800).

37.9      make . . . choking · xix.17 (800).

37.10     may . . . reign · xx.2 (800).

37.11     divers-feathered doves · xx.6 (800).

37.11–12  sweet . . . delight · xx.10 (800).

37.12     play your sports · xx.12 (801).

37.12–13  who is . . . which · xxi.1 (801).

37.13     wrought pleasures · xxi.10 (801): 'pleasures with thee wrought'.

37.14     enlarge . . . love · Apparently suggested by xxi.13 (801): 'And generation goodly dost enlarge'.

37.14     in lieu · xxiv.1 (802).

37.15     smart · xxii.6 (801).

37.15     till when · xxii.18 (801): 'Till which'.

37.15–16  to increase the count · xxiii.15 (802).

37.16     endless · xxiv.7 (802).

37.17     leave to sing · xvii.18 (799): 'leave likewise your former lay to sing'.

37.17–18  one . . . unsound · xiii.14–15 (798).

37.19 By · Byron. The references below are to *Poems* (see 4.3 n.).

37.19     mar into · *The Giaour*, 51 (154): 'mar it into'; line in margin.

37.19    shot . . . heart · *The Siege of Corinth*, xxi.35 (318): 'shot a chillness to his heart'.

38.1    a jocund morn · *Siege of Corinth*, xxii.2 (320): 'that morn were a jocund one'; cf. 38.8.

38.1    skirr the plain · *Siege of Corinth*, xxii.15 (320).

38.2 Bu · Burns. The references below are to *Poetical Works* (see 22.10 n.).

38.2    sic talents · 'To William Simpson', Postscript, ii.2 (130); cf. 38.3 with 19.6.

38.3–4    muckle din · 'To William Simpson', iv.5 (130).

38.4    loud & lang · 'To William Simpson', iv.6 (130). Cf. 38.8 with 38.1.

38.10    constellations · 'The Bonnie Wee Thing', 10 (298): 'constellation'; in TH's note the shorthand (at 38.12) = 'breasts'.

38.14    chuckie · 'To Dr. Blacklock', x.3 (175).

38.14    cockie · 'To Dr. Blacklock', x.5 (175).

38.15 Isai · Isaiah. The references below are to the Book of Isaiah, in the Bible (see 23.5 n.).

38.15    laden with · i.4; in TH's note the shorthand = 'love'.

38.15    a lodge · i.8.

38.16    to lodge in · i.21.

38.16    fed · i.11.

38.16–17    I . . . of · i.24.

38.17    turn . . . thee · i.25.

38.17–18    consume away · i.28: 'they that forsake the Lord shall be consumed'; cf. 52.8.

38.18 S.S. · Song of Solomon. The references below are to the Song of Solomon, in the Bible (see 23.5 n.).

38.18    fitly set · v.12.

38.18    a bed of spices · v.13.

39.1    dropping . . . myrrh · v.13.

39.1    set with · v.14.

39.2    overlaid · v.14.

39.2    drops of the night · v.2; underlined, line in margin.

39.3 Sh. R II · Shakespeare, *Richard II*. The references below are to *Richard II*, in vol. IV of *Dramatic Works*; those in square brackets are to *The Riverside Shakespeare* (see 3.4 n.).

39.3    the complexion of · 466.4 [III.ii.194].

39.3    I play the · 466.8 [III.ii.198].

39.4    to ear · 466.22 [III.ii.212]; footnoted.

39.4    royally · 467.24 [III.iii.21].

39.5        mann'd . . . entrance · 467.24–468.1 [III.iii.21–2]: 'mann'd, my
            lord, | Against . . .'.

39.5–6      send . . . ears · 468.12–13 [III.iii.33-4]; line in margin.

39.10       rained from · 468.23 [III.iii.44].

39.12       lay . . . with · 468.22 [III.iii.43].

39.12       unbegot · 470.16 [III.iii.88].

39.13       the testament of · 470.22 [III.iii.94]: 'The purple testament of';
            footnoted.

39.13–14    the buried . . . Gaunt · 471.12 [III.iii.109].

39.14–16    laid . . . sooth · 472.10–12 [III.iii.134–6]; footnoted.

39.17–21    I.L. . . . complain · 476.2–9 [III.iv.10–18]; footnoted. Line in
            margin beginning at '*Queen*. Of neither'.

40.1        step into · 476.16 [III.iv.25].

40.1–2      sprays . . . lofty · 477.6–7 [III.iv.34–5]; cf. 13.2

40.2        suck . . . fertility · 477.10–11 [III.iv.38–9].

40.2–3      wholesome flowers · 477.11 [III.iv.39].

40.3        is fore-run with · 476.19 [III.iv.28].

40.3–4      a pale . . . of · 477.12 [III.iv.40]: 'in the compass of a pale'.

40.4        choked up · 477.16 [III.iv.44].

40.4        unpruned · 477.17 [III.iv.45].

40.5        knots · 477.18 [III.iv.46]; footnoted.

40.5        he . . . with · 477.20–1 [III.iv.48–9]: 'He . . . | Hath now himself
            met with'.

40.6        sound these news · 478.17 [III.iv.74]: 'sound this unpleasing
            news'.

40.7        to divine · 478.22 [III.iv.79]: 'Divine'.

40.7        post you to London · 479.11 [III.iv.90].

40.8        unsay · 480.9 [IV.i.9].

40.8        if . . . sympathies · 481.18 [IV.i.33]; footnoted.

40.9        to turn . . . on · 481.24 [IV.i.39]: 'turn thy falsehood to thy
            heart'; in TH's note the shorthand = 'love'.

40.9        brandish · 482.11 [IV.i.50].

40.10       mine honour's pawn · 482.16 [IV.i.55] or 483.6 [IV.i.70]: 'my
            honour's pawn'.

40.10       to tie thee to · 483.13 [IV.i.77].

40.10–11    grant their suit · 486.13 [IV.i.154]: 'grant the commons' suit'.

40.11       figure of · 485.10 [IV.i.125].

40.11–12    a surety for · 486.18 [IV.i.159]: 'your sureties for'.

40.12       to tutor . . . submission · 487.6 [IV.i.166–7]: 'to tutor me | To
            . . .'.

40.12–13    I . . . out · 490.15 [IV.i.258].

40.13–14     a brittle glory · 491.18 [IV.i.287].

40.15 Is II · Isaiah, chap. ii. The references below are to the Book of Isaiah, in the Bible (see 23.5 n.). The significance of TH's 'ep' notation (repeated at 46.16, 47.8, and 48.3) remains unclear, the obvious 'epithets' not seeming appropriate to the actual content of the section. TH may simply be recording his use of the 'early pages' of Isaiah (in none of the four Isaiah sections does he proceed beyond chap. xi), although either 'expansions' or 'experiments' also seems possible.

40.15        exalted · ii.2.

40.16        forsaken · ii.6.

40.16        house of innocence · ii.6: 'house of Jacob'.

40.16        plenteous · Perhaps suggested by ii.6: 'replenished'; in TH's note the shorthand = 'love'.

40.17        soothsayer · ii.6: 'soothsayers'.

40.17–18     full of · ii.7.

40.18        endless · Perhaps suggested by ii.7: 'neither is there any end'.

40.18        fenced · ii.15.

40.18–19     so utterly · ii.18: 'he shall utterly'.

40.19        the captain of fifty · iii.3.

40.19–41.1   I will . . . be · iii.4; in TH's note the shorthand = 'her'.

41.1         cunningly · iii.3: 'cunning'.

41.2         provoking · iii.8: 'to provoke'.

41.2         show · iii.9.

41.2         oppressive · iii.12: 'oppressors'.

41.3         ruling · iii.12: 'rule'.

41.3         to beat to pieces · iii.15: 'beat my people to pieces'.

41.3         pleading · iii.13: 'to plead'.

41.4         excellently · iv.2: 'excellent'.

41.4         choicest · v.2.

41.4         pleasant plant · v.7.

41.5         captivitity · v.13: 'captivity'.

41.5         measureless · v.14: 'without measure'.

41.5         speeding · v.19: 'make speed'.

41.6         drawing · v.18: 'draw'.

41.6         waste place · v.17: 'waste places'; cf. 33.5.

41.8         blossom · v.24.

41.8         undone · vi.5; in TH's note the shorthand = 'love'.

41.9         purged · vi.7; cf. 21.5

41.9         wasting · vi.11: 'wasted'; in TH's note the shorthand = 'love'.

41.9         wearing · Perhaps suggested by vii.13: 'weary'; in TH's note 'fond⁸' = 'fondness'.

41.10 Sh. Rd II · Shakespeare, *Richard II.* The references below are to *Richard II,* in vol. IV of *Dramatic Works*; those in square brackets are to *The Riverside Shakespeare* (see 3.4 n.).

41.10–11    my wife . . . came · 496.12–13 [V.i.78–9].

41.11–12    and piece . . . heart · 496.26 [V.i.92].

41.12    Kill thy heart · 497.6 [V.i.98].

41.13 Sc. Kenil · Scott, *Kenilworth.* The references below are to volume, page, and line number of *Kenilworth,* 2 vols. (Edinburgh: Robert Cadell; London: Whittaker & Co., 1831), being vols. XXII and XXIII of the 'magnum opus' edition of the Waverley Novels (43 vols., Edinburgh and London, 1829–31). *Kenilworth* is one of the titles missing from the broken set of the Waverley Novels as issued in 25 parts (Edinburgh: Adam and Charles Black, 1866–8) which was once in TH's possession and is now in the National Library of Scotland. Given within square brackets are the relevant chapter numbers as they appear in one-volume editions of the novel.

41.13    conjure away · XXII.19.8 [chap. 1]: 'conjure them away'.

41.13    lay them · XXII.19.9 [chap. 1]: 'laying them'.

41.13–14    swathed . . . wisp · XXII.19.15–16 [chap. 1].

41.14    whimpering · XXII.36.2 [chap. 3].

41.14    defoul · XXII.36.5 [chap. 1].

41.15    parry advice · XXII.37.27 [chap. 3]: 'parry the advice'.

41.15    taking . . . woman · XXII.60.15 [chap. 4]: 'take the wall of her'.

41.16    the full . . . dignity · XXII.86.15 [chap. 5].

41.17    a champion . . . outrance · XXII.104.4–5 [chap. 6]: 'a champion of that same naked virtue called truth, to the very outrance'.

41.17    spell . . . splendour · XXII.110.31–111.1 [chap. 7]; cf. 13.5, 14.16.

42.1    court or congregation · XXII.118.30–1 [chap. 7]: 'the court, . . . the congregation'.

42.1    probing · XXII.227.3 [chap. 12].

42.1    feast · XXII.230.8 [chap. 12].

42.2    pay · XXII.230.2 [chap. 12].

42.2    alchemy · Perhaps suggested by the chap. 13 epigraph at XXII.234.7 from Jonson's *The Alchemist,* although 'alchemy' itself (spelled 'alchymy') first appears at XXII.190.9 [chap. 10].

42.2    this light o' love · XXIII.60.25 [chap. 21].

42.3    had hurt . . . her · XXIII.69.16 [chap. 22]: 'had much hurt his . . .'.

42.4 Sc. L of I · Scott, *The Lord of the Isles.* The references below are to *The Lord of the Isles,* in *Poetical Works* (see 4.1 n.).

42.4    a milder pang · II.iv.4 (421).

42.4–5    to chafe thee · II.xiv.10 (423).

42.5    in minstrel line · II.xviii.7 (424).

42.6 Jer: II · Jeremiah, chap. ii. The references below are to the Book of Jeremiah, in the Bible (see 23.5 n.). 'id.' = perhaps TH's abbreviation for 'idioms' or 'idiomatic'.

42.6          Cry . . . of · ii.2.

42.6–8        they . . . vanity · ii.5.

42.8          found in me · ii.5.

42.8–9        they . . . law · ii.8.

42.9–10       walk . . . profit · ii.8: 'walked after . . .'.

42.10         plead with · ii.9.

42.10–11      thine . . . me · ii.22: 'thine iniquity . . .'.

42.11         gaddest thou · ii.36; cf. 35.10.

42.11–12      In . . . them · iii.2.

42.12         put away · iv.1.

42.12–13      turned unto me · iii.10.

42.13         to fall upon you · iii.12.

42.13–14      shall . . . Israel · iii.18.

42.14         put thee among · iii.19.

42.14–15      publish against · iv.16.

42.15         give out against · iv.16: 'give out their voice against'.

42.16 Barnes · William Barnes. The references below are to stanza, line, and (in parentheses) page number of *Poems of Rural Life in the Dorset Dialect. Third Collection* (London: John Russell Smith, 1862). Barnes's three separately published collections of Dorset dialect poems were not brought together into a single, finally revised volume until the publication of *Poems of Rural Life in the Dorset Dialect* (London: C. Kegan Paul) in 1879. TH, compiling his notebook in the mid-1860s, consulted both this first edition of the Third Collection and a revised edition of the First Collection (see below, 43.16 n.). TH had known Barnes in Dorchester in the 1850s (see *Life*, 32, 502), but it was not until the mid-1870s that they met as literary equals.

42.18         rim · 'Woone Smile Mwore', i.2 (1).

42.18         shrinken moss · 'Woone Smile Mwore', ii.3 (1): 'shrinkèn moss'; cf. 68.3.

42.18–19      the leanen apple tree · 'Woone Smile Mwore', ii.4 (1): 'the leänèn apple tree'.

42.19         his bow'd tail · 'Woone Smile Mwore', ii.6 (2): 'His low-bow'd taïl'.

42.19         sprack · 'Woone Smile Mwore', iii.1 (2).

43.1          her shade . . . black · 'Woone Smile Mwore', iii.3 (2): 'her sheäde, a-whiv'rèn black'; cf. 44.1.

43.1          overright · 'The Echo', i.2 (3).

43.2          avore · 'The Echo', i.4 (3); cf. 44.2.

43.2          slooe · 'The Echo', ii.4 (3).

43.2        back in May · 'The Echo', iii.2 (3): 'back in Mäy'.

43.3 Jer V & VI · Jeremiah, chaps. v and vi. The references below are to the Book of Jeremiah, in the Bible (see 23.5 n.). For 'id' see 42.6 n.

43.3        Are . . . truth · v.3; in TH's note the shorthand = 'love'.

43.4        to the full · v.7.

43.5        given to · vi.13.

43.5        to try · vi.27: 'try'.

43.6 Dic · Dictionary. See 35.9 n., although TH's concentration here on words beginning with 'b' is suggestive of the systematic lexical exploration also reflected in his extensive marking of words beginning with 'd' in his copy of Nuttall. See also 45.1 and n. and 46.5 and n. Cf. 43.7–8 with 20.8. The 'b' at the end of the entry is TH's memorandum of the point in the alphabet at which he broke off.

43.11 Sc · Scott. The references below are to *The Lord of the Isles*, in *Poetical Works* (see 4.1 n.).

43.11       show · II.xviii.16 (424): 'Show'd'.

43.11       to wind through · II.xxii.2–3 (425): 'through the wide revolving door | The black-stoled brethren wind'.

43.11–12    o'er . . . convulsions · II.xxx.3–4 (428): 'o'er his pallid features . . .'.

43.12       bore away · II.xxxii.37 (429).

43.13       a silence . . . wood · III.i.3–4 (429).

43.14       drew to · III.vii.5 (430): 'Draws to'.

43.14       the winter worn o'er · III.ix.9 (431): 'The winter worn in exile o'er'.

43.15       to sway · III.x.19 (431): 'Shalt sway'.

43.16 Barnes · The references below are to stanza, line, and (in parentheses) page number of *Poems of Rural Life in the Dorset Dialect. First Collection*, 3rd edn. (London: John Russell Smith, 1862). For TH and Barnes see above, 42.16 n. The two earlier editions of this Collection, in 1844 and 1848, both include, as the 1862 does not, an introductory 'Dissertation on the Dorset Dialect' and a glossary of dialect words. Textual discrepancies make it clear that TH did not use the edition of 1844; he could have used the 1848 edition, but his spelling (e.g. 'cwoffer' at 44.2) suggests that he was following the more 'standardized' forms of the 1862. After TH's death Florence Hardy presented to E. M. Forster a copy (King's College, Cambridge) of this latter edition which TH had used in preparing his own edition, *Select Poems of William Barnes* (London: Henry Frowde, 1908), but it was evidently not in TH's possession in the 1860s.

43.16       the grægle's bell · 'The Spring', ii.4 (1): 'the wood-screen'd grægle's bell'.

43.16       sky-blue · 'The Spring', ii.5 (1).

43.17       to fay wrong · 'The Spring', iv.2 (2): 'Things all faÿ wrong'.

43.17 underneath the showers · 'The Woodlands', i.3 (2): 'underneath the dewy show'rs'.

43.17 drong · 'The Woodlands', i.5 (2).

44.1 whivered · 'The Woodlands', iii.1 (3): 'whiver'd'; cf. 43.1.

44.1 my memory . . . good · 'The Woodlands', iv.7 (3): 'My memory shall meäke em good'.

44.2 a staddle · 'Leady-day, an' Ridden House', 24 (4): 'woone wold staddle'.

44.2 avore · 'Leady-day, an' Ridden House', 25 (4); cf. 43.2

44.2 cwoffer · 'Leady-day, an' Ridden House', 34 (5).

44.2 the reaves · 'Leady-day, an' Ridden House', 46 (5): 'the reäves'.

44.3 athirt · 'Leady-day, an' Ridden House', 54 (5).

44.3 settle · 'Leady-day, an' Ridden House', 58 (5).

44.3 fusty · 'Leady-day, an' Ridden House', 76 (6).

44.3 a tutty · 'Easter Zunday', i.6 (7).

44.4 kitty-boots · 'Easter Zunday', i.11 (7).

44.4 spry · 'Easter Monday', i.5 (8).

44.4 a tait · 'Easter Monday', ii.7 (8): 'a taït'.

44.5 Jer · Jeremiah. The references below are to the Book of Jeremiah, in the Bible (see 23.5 n.). For 'id' see 42.6 n.

44.5 to your hurt · vii.6.

44.5 to set . . . name · vii.12: 'I set my name'.

44.6 lift up a cry · vii.16: 'lift up cry'.

44.6 make . . . h. · vii.18: '. . . of heaven'.

44.7 see . . . it · vii.12.

44.8 to be well with · vii.23: 'may be well unto'.

44.8 take up a lamentation · vii.29.

44.9 came . . . heart · vii.31: 'came it into . . .'.

44.9 to fray away · vii.33: 'shall fray them away'.

44.9-10 to spread before · viii.2: 'shall spread them before'.

44.10 slidden back · viii.5.

44.10 given to · viii.10.

44.11 to put to silence · viii.14: 'hath put us to silence'.

44.11-12 is . . . Zion · viii.19: 'Is not the Lord in Zion? is not her king in her?'

44.12 the hurt · viii.21.

44.12-13 astonish[t] . . . me · viii.21: 'astonishment hath . . .'.

44.13 a lodging place · ix.2.

44.13 wayfaring · ix.2.

44.14 to know thy mind · ix.6: 'to know me'.

44.14 to do for · ix.7: 'shall I do for'.

44.14–15    gloomy . . . for · ix.8: 'layeth his wait'.

44.15    visit upon · ix.9: 'visit'; also 'visit upon' in marginal note to ix.25.

44.15    to cut off · ix.21; in TH's note the shorthand = 'love, hope'.

44.16    to fall upon · ix.22: 'shall fall as dung upon'.

44.16    glory in · ix.23; in TH's note the shorthand = 'love'.

44.17    let . . . this · ix.24.

44.18    to delight in · ix.24: 'in these things I delight'. 'ix' = TH's memorandum of the chapter at which he broke off.

45.1 Dic · Dictionary. See 43.6 n. The shorthand at 45.9 = 'love'; the 'c' at the end of the entry is TH's memorandum of the point in the alphabet at which he broke off.

45.13 F. Q. · *The Faerie Queene*. The references below are to *The Faerie Queene* (see 4.12 n.).

45.13    it fortuned · Book I, III.v.1 (23).

45.13    to weld or wield · For 'weld' see, e.g., Book I, XI.xxviii.8 (114); for 'wield' (with line in margin) see, e.g., Book I, IV.xi.6 (33).

45.13–14    cries . . . forth · Book I, VI.vi.2 (54): 'Does throw out thrilling shriekes, and shrieking cryes'.

45.14    to play about · Book II, VI.vii.8–9 (180): 'play | About'.

45.15 Sha · Shakespeare. The references below are to *Richard III*, in vol. VI of *Dramatic Works*; those in square brackets are to *The Riverside Shakespeare* (see 3.4 n.).

45.15–16    dew . . . blade · 549.6 [V.iii.181]: 'Cold fearful drops stand on my trembling flesh'.

45.16    to use sins · 549.23 [V.iii.198]: 'sins, all us'd'.

45.16–17    every . . . tale · 549.19 [V.iii.194]; cf. 30.16.

45.17    has . . . salutation · 550.4 [V.iii.210]: 'Hath twice . . .'.

45.18    dreams . . . in · 550.21–2 [V.iii.227–8].

45.18    the foe . . . field · 553.9 [V.iii.288].

46.1    to cope with · 554.11 [V.iii.315]: 'to cope withal'; cf. 22.18.

46.1–2    amaze the welkin · 555.13 [V.iii.341]; footnoted.

46.3 Buch · Robert Buchanan. The references below are to page and line number of *Idyls and Legends of Inverburn* (London: Alexander Strahan, 1865).

46.3    to think . . . puzzle · 'The English Huswife's Gossip', 75.20: 'To think the puzzle out'.

46.4    stale · Not found in verse or prose published by Buchanan prior to 1869.

46.4    to fleet · 'White Lily of Weardale-Head', 69.11: 'fleet'; cf. 19.6.

46.4 By · Byron. The reference below is to *The Complete Poetical Works. Volume V: Don Juan*, ed. Jerome J. McGann (Oxford: Clarendon Press, 1986). TH seems not to have owned a copy of *Don Juan*.

46.4      to see into · I.xxxix.2 (21): 'saw into herself'.

46.5 Dic · Dictionary. See 43.6 n. The shorthand at 46.7 and 46.8 = 'love'; the 'g' at the end of the entry is TH's memorandum of the point in the alphabet at which he broke off.

46.16 Is · Isaiah. The references below are to the Book of Isaiah, in the Bible (see 23.5 n.). For 'ep' see 40.15 n.

46.16     confederate charms · vii.2 : 'Syria is confederate with Ephraim'.

46.16     taken against me · vii.5: 'taken evil counsel against thee'.

46.17     my . . . hope · vii.18: 'the uttermost part of the rivers of Egypt'.

46.18–19  desolate . . . body · vii.19: 'desolate valleys'.

46.19     nourishing . . . sweetness · vii.21: 'a man shall nourish a young cow'.

47.1–2    abundant . . . blushes · vii.22: 'abundance of milk'; shorthand = 'love'.

47.2      loving-place · vii.23: 'place'.

47.2      briars · vii.23; cf. 48.15.

47.3      the mattock · vii.25.

47.3–4    if years . . . fail · viii.2: 'I took unto me faithful witnesses'.

47.4      the familiar thought · viii.19: 'familiar spirits'.

47.5      a peeping hope · viii.19: 'wizards that peep'.

47.5      cheeks . . . red · viii.19: 'the living to the dead'; cf. 62.10. '8' = TH's memorandum of the chapter at which he broke off.

47.7      it cannot stand · viii.10: 'it shall not stand'. Despite the square brackets this entry is not a TH invention but an addition, with the next entry, to the block of citations from Isaiah viii.

47.7      took to me · viii.2: 'took unto me'.

47.8 Is · Isaiah. The references below are to the Book of Isaiah, in the Bible (see 23.5 n.). For 'ep' see 40.15 n.

47.8      the nations · ix.3: 'the nation'.

47.9      shiny · ix.2: 'light shined'.

47.9      you . . . tears · ix.3: 'Thou hast multiplied the nation'.

47.9      to joy · ix.3: 'joy'.

47.9–10   the yoke of loneliness · ix.4: 'the yoke of his burden'; cf. 47.16.

47.10     stoutness · ix.9.

47.10     destroying years · ix.16: 'they that are led of them are destroyed'.

47.11     lifting joy · ix.18: 'lifting up of smoke'.

47.11     needy heart · x.2: 'the needy'; cf. 48.4–6.

47.11     robbing time · x.2: 'rob the fatherless'.

47.11–12  those excelling times · x.10: 'graven images did excel'.

47.12     the glory . . . looks · x.12.

47.13     [shorthand] . . . time · x.13: 'I have put down the inhabitants'; shorthand = 'love'.

47.13       a valiant man · x.13.

47.13       leanness · x.16.

47.14       kindle a burning · x.16.

47.14       his fruitful field · x.18.

47.14       a standard bearer · x.18.

47.15       few . . . them · x.19.

47.15–16    an over-flowing heart · x.22: 'the consumption decreed shall overflow with righteousness'; cf. 47.19.

47.16       our determined [shorthand] · x.23: 'a consumption, even determined'; shorthand = 'love'. Cf. 47.19.

47.16       yoking [shorthand] · x.27: 'his yoke from off thy neck'; shorthand = 'love'. Cf. 47.9–10.

47.17       the anointing . . . words · x.27: 'the yoke shall be destroyed because of the anointing'.

47.17–18    shake . . . against · x.32.

47.18       laid up thought · x.28: 'laid up his carriages'.

47.18       lopped my hope · x.33: 'lop the bough'. 'x' = TH's memorandum of the chapter to which he should, and did, return.

47.19       such determined sweetness · x.23: 'a consumption, even determined'; cf. 47.16.

47.19       flowing sweetness · x.22: 'shall overflow with righteousness'; cf. 47.15–16.

48.1–2      as my . . . age · Perhaps suggested by x.23: 'the Lord God of hosts shall make a consumption'.

48.3 Is · Isaiah. The references below are to the Book of Isaiah, in the Bible (see 23.5 n.). For 'ep' see 40.15 n.

48.3        woe unto kisses · x.1: 'Woe unto them'.

48.3–4      to turn . . . me · x.2: 'To turn aside the needy'.

48.4–6      needy . . . beauty · x.2: 'the needy'; cf. 47.11.

48.6–7      my . . . on · Perhaps suggested by x.2: 'fatherless'.

48.7–8      bowed . . . [shorthand] · x.4: 'bow down under the prisoners'; shorthand = 'love'.

48.8        if . . . under · x.4: 'they shall fall under'.

48.8–9      [shorthand] . . . thing · Apparently a TH invention; shorthand = 'love'.

48.9        a kingly thought · Perhaps suggested by x.7: 'think', and x.8: 'kings'. Cf. 16.8.

48.9–10     the fruit of · x.12.

48.10       stout resolve · x.12: 'stout heart'; cf. 11.15, 48.13.

48.10–11    high fondness · x.12: 'high looks'.

48.11       prudent brained fondness · x.13: 'by my wisdom; for I am prudent'.

48.11–2    that . . . heart · x.13: 'their treasures'.

48.12–15   hewers . . . sweetest · x.15: 'Shall the ax boast itself against him that heweth'; cf. 11.15, 48.10.

48.15–16   those . . . hope · x.17: 'it shall burn and devour his thorns and his briers'; cf. 47.2.

48.16–17   my . . . gone · x.20: 'the remnant of Israel'; 'remnant' also occurs in x.21 and x.22. Cf. 52.10.

48.17      smiting · x.24 or xi.4: 'shall smite'.

48.17      virtues, "the outcasts · xi.12: 'the outcasts'.

48.18      eyes . . . speech · xi.15: 'his mighty wind'. 'XI' = TH's memorandum of the chapter in which he broke off.

49.1 Lucr · Lucretius. The references below are to page and line number of the prose version of Book I of *Lucretius on the Nature of Things. A Philosophical Poem*, trans. John Selby Watson (London: Henry G. Bohn, 1851). TH's copy (Colby) contains numerous pencil annotations and markings.

49.1       the gliding constellations · 2.2.

49.1–2     unveil . . . day · 3.6–7: 'the vernal face of day is unveiled'.

49.3       spring . . . life · 3.19–20: 'spring into the ethereal realms of light'.

49.3       fling . . . at · 4.8–9: 'flings himself upon'.

49.4       crisis . . . heat · 5.6: 'at such a crisis'. It appears from the preceding passage in Lucretius that TH's 'heat' may be a slip for 'heart'.

49.4       this system of pain · 5.12–13: 'the whole system of heaven'.

49.5 1 Sam. 26. · 1 Samuel, chap. xxvi. TH's quotations, however, are from chap. xxvii of the First Book of Samuel, in the Bible (see 23.5 n.); chap. xxvi was evidently his starting-point.

49.5       to tell on, upon · xxvii.11: 'should tell on'.

49.5–6     said in my heart · xxvii.1: 'said in his heart'.

49.7 Swin · Swinburne. The references below are to stanza, line, and (in parentheses) page number of *Poems and Ballads* (London: Edward Moxon, 1866).

49.7       the thing . . . seen · 'A Ballad of Burdens', v.4 (145).

49.7–8     from the . . . Ida · 'Dolores', xlii.5 (191); cf. 28.4.

49.8–9     I shall . . . roses · 'The Triumph of Time', xlv.1 (53).

49.13      overblown · 'Dolores', x.6 (181).

49.13      bared . . . to · 'Dolores', xiii.2 (182).

49.13      fain · 'Dolores', xiii.6 (182); cf. 15.15, 29.10.

49.15–18   As the . . . lift · 'Satia te Sanguine', iii.1–4 (98). The asterisks added at the end of lines 15 and 17 are similar to those habitually used by TH in later years to locate points in his manuscripts at which additional material was to be introduced; here, however, he seems simply to be registering the rhyming of 'limbs' and 'swims'.

49.19      You kill . . . hearts · 'Satia te Sanguine', xii.4 (100).

49.19      carve · 'Satia te Sanguine', xiv.3 (100).

49.20      whet · 'Satia te Sanguine', xiv.4 (100).

49.20      dumb . . . dart · 'Satia te Sanguine', xv.2 (100).

49.20–1    on this wise · 'A Litany', Seventh Antiphone, 2 (104).

49.21      gone thorough · 'A Lamentation', I.i.10 (108).

49.21      a privy way · 'The Leper', viii.2 (138).

50.1       eyelids . . . purple · 'The Leper', xxvii.3–4 (141): 'eyelids madden me, | That were shot . . .'.

50.1       comelier · 'The Leper', xiii.1 (139).

50.2       feet . . . mire · 'A Cameo', 8 (130): 'feet unshod that pashed . . .'.

50.2–3     earth . . . her · 'Before Dawn', i.2 (174).

50.3       fates · 'Rondel', i.3 (97).

50.4       lids · 'Ilicet', ii.3 (85).

50.4–5     the stooped urn, (dipping) · 'Ilicet', ix.1 (87): 'The stooped urn, filling, dips'.

50.5       sad blosoms · 'Ilicet', xi.4 (87): 'sad red blossoms'.

50.5       the slow blood · See next entry.

50.6       the slow . . . blood · 'Ilicet', xiii.3 (88).

50.6–7     bathing the spices · 'Ilicet', xiii.4 (88).

50.7–8     drink . . . reddened · 'Ilicet', xiv.2 (88).

50.8       the date of us · 'Ilicet', xviii.3 (89): 'the date of all of us'.

50.9       trapped · 'Ilicet', xxi.1 (89).

50.9       iron sides falter · 'Ilicet', xxii.1 (90): 'iron sides of the old world falter'.

50.9       periods · 'Ilicet', xxii.3 (90).

50.10      latter men · 'Ilicet', xxii.5 (90).

50.10      lift up thy lips · 'Hermaphroditus', i.1 (91); the shorthand in TH's note = 'love'.

50.14–15   Of all . . . of · 'Hermaphroditus', i.2–3 (91).

50.16      A pleasure house · 'Hermaphroditus', ii.10 (92).

50.16–17   in what swift wise · 'Hermaphroditus', iv.9 (93).

50.17      sometime · 'St. Dorothy', 6 (274); cf. 11.11, 15.6.

50.18–19   I know . . . hair · 'Before Parting', vi.1 (213). Cf. 51.1 with 63.10.

51.1–2     love . . . pleasure · 'Before Parting', vi.5 (213).

51.2       that has no heart · 'A Ballad of Burdens', i.4 (144).

51.3 Ezek: 27 · Ezekiel, chap. xxvii. The reference below is to the Book of Ezekiel, in the Bible (see 23.5 n.).

51.3       the event . . . me · xxvii.1: 'The word of the Lord came again unto me'.

51.4 Ezek I · Ezekiel, chap. i. The references below are to the Book of Ezekiel, in the Bible (see 23.5 n.).

51.4–5     I . . . dreams · i.1: 'I was among the captives'; shorthand = 'love'.

51.5–6     the hand . . . me · i.3: 'the hand of the Lord was there upon him'; shorthand = 'love'.

51.7       a delight . . . it · i.4: 'a brightness was about it'.

51.7–8     went . . . among · i.13.

51.8       'twas as it were · i.16: 'their work was as it were'.

51.8–9     so . . . mournful · i.18: 'so high that they were dreadful'.

51.9       when . . . for · i.18: 'their rings were full of eyes round about them four'.

51.10      wherever . . . me · Apparently a fusion, and variation, of i.20: 'Whithersoever the spirit was to go', and i.19: 'the wheels went by them'.

51.10      went · i.21.

51.10      stood · i.21.

51.11      it had . . . it · Perhaps i.21: 'the spirit of the living creature was in the wheels'.

51.11–12   doubts are with me · ii.6: 'though briers and thorns be with thee'.

51.12      I . . . to h. · Apparently iii.5: 'thou art not sent to a people'.

51.13–15   I . . . [shorthand] · iii.8: 'I have made thy face strong against their faces'; shorthand = 'lips'.

51.15–16   I . . . thought · iii.10: 'all my words that I shall speak unto thee receive in thine heart'.

51.16      strong upon me · iii.14.

51.16–17   it came . . . c. · iii.16: 'the word of the Lord came unto me'.

51.17–19   [shorthand] . . . night · iii.17: 'I have made thee a watchman unto the house of Israel'; shorthand = 'love'.

51.19–52.1 I . . . eyes · iii.18: 'his blood will I require at thine hand'; shorthand = 'love'.

52.1       to turn from [shorthand] · iii.19: 'turn not from his wickedness'; shorthand = 'love'.

52.1–3     might . . . him · Perhaps iii.25: 'thou shalt not go out among them'; cf. 52.8–10.

52.3–4     my . . . scourge · iii.26: 'thou . . . shalt not be to them a reprover'.

52.4–5     I laid . . . me · iii.20: 'I lay a stumblingblock before him'.

52.5       cast . . . me · iv.2: 'cast a mount against it'.

52.5–6     to set against · iv.2: 'set the camp also against'; see also following verse.

52.6       to lay upon one · iv.5: 'have laid upon thee'.

52.7       to lay out to · Apparently suggested by the preceding entry.

52.7        drove . . . away · Apparently suggested by iv.13: 'whither I will drive them'.

52.8        consume away · iv.17; cf. 38.17–18.

52.8        you will . . . me · v.8: 'I, even I, am against thee'.

52.8–10     thou wilt . . . then · Perhaps iii.25: 'thou shalt not go out among them'; cf. 48.16, 52.1–3.

52.10–11    I rest upon you · v.13: 'I will cause my fury to rest upon them'.

52.11       unsparing eyes · v.11: 'neither shall mine eye spare'.

52.11–12    the last . . . soul · v.12: 'A third part of thee shall die with the pestilence'.

52.12–13    when . . . mine · Apparently suggested by the preceding entry.

52.13–14    when . . . me · v.13: 'when I have accomplished my fury in them'; in TH's note the shorthand = 'love'.

52.14–15    lay . . . days · v.14: 'I will make thee waste'.

52.15–16    an astonishment to them · v.15: 'an astonishment unto the nations'.

52.16       send upon me the · v.16: 'send upon them the'.

52.17       a flit . . . me · v.17: 'pestilence and blood shall pass through thee'. 'VI' = TH's memorandum (expanded from the original 'V') of the point at which he should resume.

52.19 Swin · Swinburne. The references below are to page and line number of the second edition of *Atalanta in Calydon. A Tragedy* (London: Edward Moxon, 1865). Since only one hundred copies of the first edition were printed, TH is unlikely to have seen it. References in square brackets are to page and line number of vol. VII of the Bonchurch Edition (see 20.2 n.).

52.19       leave thee · 21.5 [281.27].

53.1–2      sisters . . . arrow · 23.16, 24.1–2 [283.15, 17–18]: '. . . fawns | Who feed . . .'.

53.2        at whiles · 24.2 [283.18].

53.3        she . . . kisses her · 24.6, 7 [283.22, 23].

53.4        savours · 25.4 [284.8].

53.4        lands . . . summer · 29.19 [287.12].

53.5        unfooted ways · 29.20 [287.13].

53.5        at one with · 28.10 [286.12].

53.5        thankworthy · 31.22 [288.23].

53.6        unleashed · 32.10 [288.33].

53.6        seen otherwise · 33.16 [289.24].

53.6–8      wild . . . streams · 34.20–1 [290.17–18].

53.8–9      for silver . . . whiter · 38.9–10 [292.25–6].

53.10       an evil blossom · 41.1 [294.11].

53.11–18    For an . . . years · 41.1–8 [294.11–18].

54.1        thunder of storm · 44.21 [296.29].

54.1–2      wailing of wives · 45.1 [296.30: Bonchurch edn. reads 'waves'].

54.2        clamour of currents · 45.9 [297.6].

54.2        eyeshot · 48.3 [298.29].

54.3        the first of the morning · 53.22 [302.21].

54.4        rise . . . not · 55.8 [303.16].

54.4        Would God · 54.12 [302.33].

54.5        nor the spoil . . . fame · 55.13 [303.21].

54.6        who gives . . . away · 61.21 [307.21]; cf. 57.8.

54.6–7      Meleager . . . leaf · 67.17–18 [311.15–16].

54.8–10     the green . . . untunable · 68.22–69.1 [312.7–8].

54.10       up in heaven · 60.1 [306.15].

54.10–11    much . . . him · 69.7 [312.14].

54.12       bride-bound to the gods · 68.2 [311.20].

54.13       they saw . . . scented · 68.18 [312.3]. '[Admis.]' = 'Admissible',
            i.e. an allowable construction.

54.13–14    the sudden string · 69.16 [312.23].

54.14       the waterish air · 69.17 [312.24].

54.15       tense · 69.21 [312.28]; cf. 8.2.

54.15–16    the roar . . . streams · 70.20 [313.17].

54.18       blossoms . . . sod · 74.5 [315.17].

54.18–19    to brush . . . [shorthand] · Apparently suggested by 74.10–11
            [315.22–3]: 'brush the bare | Snow-soft shoulders of a god'.
            Shorthand = 'cheek' and 'lip, kiss, robe'.

54.19–55.1  hours . . . noon · 74.14–15 [315.26–7]: 'hours, | Those that . . .'.

55.1–2      shall . . . day · 98.4 [330.16].

55.2–3      out . . . rainiest · 101.12 [333.5].

55.3        kinship · 124.3 [347.16].

55.5–57.18  But up . . . God · 60.1–62.10 [306.15–307.31]; cf. 54.6, 74.9.

58.1 Sc · Scott. The references below are to *The Lord of the Isles*, in *Poetical Works* (see 4.1 n.).

58.1        amid . . . conquest-cry · IV.xx.6 (445).

58.1–3      to meaner . . . mind · IV.xxii.25–6 (446); cf. 4.4.

58.3        whence that light? · V.xvii.1 (454): 'whence that wondrous light'.

58.4        the sound . . . sea · V.xix.5 (455).

58.4–5      a glade . . . alleys · V.xix.12–13 (455): 'a glade between, |
            Whose tangled alleys'.

58.5        faintly blue · V.vii.13 (451); in TH's note the shorthand =
            'cheek' and 'eyes', the latter an incorrect symbol repeated and
            then amended at 60.4.

58.7 Swin. Chast · Swinburne, *Chastelard*. The references below are to *Chastelard*; those in square brackets are to the Bonchurch Edition (see 20.2 n.).

58.7–9    I think . . . them · 38.1–3 [27.9–11].

58.10    point . . . him · 39.18 [28.15].

58.11–16    Queen . . . him · 118.9–14 [72.10–15].

58.17–59.4    Finding . . . successf: · See *Life*, 34–5, and *Biography*, 64: TH is recalling an occasion, apparently in 1860, when he had grudgingly missed a circus parade in Dorchester in order to attend a prayer-meeting, as agreed with his friends Alfred and William Perkins (sons of the local Baptist minister), only to be left waiting until the Perkinses arrived after having themselves watched the parade. As noted in the Introduction (xiv–xv), the reference to 'cutting Architecture if successful' appears to be inverted by one of the partially erased (and apparently later) notes on the rear endpaper.

59.5–8    Now three . . . well · 186.13–16 [113.23–6].

59.9–10    Her name . . . written · 21.9–10 [16.19–20].

59.10–11    I know . . . much · 21.10–11 [16.20–21]; cf. 5.4, 32.6.

59.11    to gird at · 21.16 [17.1]; cf. 21.19.

59.11    meseems · 24.15 [18.19].

59.11–12    face . . . cheeks · 33.4–5 [24.7–8].

59.13    flowertime · 33.7 [24.10].

59.13    the supple . . . hath · 35.2 [25.15].

59.14    sky colour · 39.4 [28.1].

59.15    a saintship · 40.4 [28.18].

59.15    laced · 41.8 [29.8].

59.15–16    some . . . lips · 42.9–10 [29.24–5].

59.17    sweeter . . . life · 87.11 [54.22].

59.17–18    love . . . flesh · 101.1 [63.4].

59.19    enbloom · Apparently a TH invention; the word is not in *OED*.

60.2 Thes · Thesaurus. Although Roget's *Thesaurus* had appeared in 1852, TH seems to be using the term 'thesaurus' in its general sense of 'A "treasury" or "storehouse" of knowledge' (*OED*). He perhaps compiled this list by going through a dictionary in sequential but otherwise random fashion, recording finally the letter of the alphabet at which he had broken off (cf. 63.7, 66.7). '(adjs) & (subs.)' = 'adjectives and substantives'. The shorthand at 60.4 = 'eyes', at 60.18 = 'etting' (TH's arbitrary symbol to complete 'besetting'), at 61.19 = 'love', at 62.5 = 'love', at 62.8 = 'cheek', at 62.10 = 'kisses', at 62.13 = 'love', and at 62.15 = 'love'. Cf. 61.3–4 with 35.2–3; 62.2 and 62.12 with 9.3; and 62.10 with 47.5.

62.16 Rickm · Thomas Rickman. The references below are to page and line number of *An Attempt to Discriminate the Styles of Architecture in England, from the Conquest to the Reformation*, 6th edn. (Oxford and London: John Henry and James Parker, 1862). For Rickman's career, see H. M. Colvin, *A Biographical Dictionary of English Architects, 1660–1840* (London: John Murray, 1954), 498–501; he is briefly mentioned in *A Laodicean* (Wessex Edn.), 6.

62.16    the set of thy head · 261.10–11: 'two sets of mouldings'.

62.16–17    fine-drawn kisses · 261.6: 'fine hollow mouldings'.

62.17    sweep of lip · 261.14: 'sweep of mouldings'.

62.17–18    soft . . . mouth · Apparently TH inventions.

62.19    sweet . . . feasts · 262.1–2: 'bell of the capital'.

63.1    flowered braids · 262.3: 'flowered capitals'.

63.1    curly . . . hair · 261.14–15: 'set up lengthways'.

63.1–2    eyes . . . execution · 262.12–13: 'west doorways of York are of the richest execution'.

63.2    worked pale by k—— · See next entry.

63.3    carved . . . neck · 262.14: 'open-work bands'.

63.3–4    fragile sobs · 262.14–15: 'ornament equally beautiful, and not so fragile'.

63.4    profuse swee— · 263.2–3: 'in great profusion'.

63.4–5    canopies of thy eyes · 263.4: 'canopies'.

63.5    drip of tears · 263.4: 'dripstone'.

63.5–6    coming . . . breast · 263.5–6: 'a plain return'.

63.6    the finish of thy face · 263.12: 'is finished'.

63.7 Thes & Sw · Thesaurus and Swinburne. For 'Thes' see 60.2 n. Cf. 63.10 with 51.1. The Swinburne references at 63.11–17 are to *Poems and Ballads* (see 49.7 n.).

63.11    the dewfall · 'An Interlude', ix.3 (231); cf. 17.6.

63.11-12    lightened with laughter · 'An Interlude', iii.3 (230).

63.12–13    And May . . . flower · 'An Interlude', xii.1 (232).

63.15    the month . . . roses · 'Hendecasyllabics', 1 (233).

63.17    The head of a smile · Apparently a TH invention.

63.18 Swin · Swinburne. The references below are to *Poems and Ballads* (see 49.7 n.). Shorthand = 'omit' but 'imitate' (cf. 66.3) perhaps intended.

63.19    kissed out · 'Before Parting', vi.5 (213).

63.19    August blue · 'The Sundew', ix.4 (216).

63.19    green miles · 'The Sundew', vii.2 (215).

64.1 Swin · Swinburne. The references below are to *Poems and Ballads* (see 49.7 n.).

64.2    pricked . . . red · 'The Sundew', i.2 (214).

64.2    jets · 'The Sundew', i.4 (214).

64.3    deep scent · 'The Sundew', iii.1 (214).

64.5–66.2    O brother . . . know? · 'The Triumph of Time', xliii–xliv, xlviii–xlix (53–5). At 64.11 TH has 'gives' for 'gave' (xliii.7) and at 65.3 'comes' for 'came' (xliv.8).

66.3 A mirth · The quotation is from *Antony and Cleopatra*, in *Dramatic Works* (see 3.4 n.), X.199.8 [*Riverside Shakespeare*, I.iv.18]. Shorthand = 'imitate'.

66.4 Swin · Swinburne. The references below are to *Poems and Ballads* (see 49.7 n.).

66.4        beyond · 'Before Dawn', iii.3 and iii.4 (175).

66.4        years fell past · 'The Triumph of Time', vi.6 (41).

66.5        fair . . . grey · 'A Ballad of Burdens', i.5 (144).

66.6        lithe · 'Faustine', xviii.2 (125); cf. 15.10.

66.6        pores · 'Faustine', xviii.3 (125).

66.6        dew of lip · 'Faustine', xxvi.3 (126): 'lips were dashed with dew'.

66.7 Thes · Thesaurus. See 60.2 n. At 67.2 'far' = TH's memorandum of the word at which he broke off.

67.3–4 Carl. Dan · Carlyle's Dante. The references below are to *Dante's Divine Comedy: The Inferno. A Literal Prose Translation, with the Text of the Original* . . ., trans. John A. Carlyle (London: Chapman and Hall, 1849). TH perhaps used the second printing of 1867; he certainly purchased and used at a later date a copy of the 1882 printing (now in DCM): see *LitN*, II.566.

67.3–4        the fear . . . look · 6 n. 2.

67.4        between . . . Feltro · 10.4–5; footnoted.

67.5        quits . . . commenced · 16.11; footnoted.

67.6        with thinking . . . enterprise · 17.1–2.

67.7–8        so fair . . . command · 17.12–18.1.

67.8        single in worth · 19.13.

67.8–9        flowerets . . . them · 23.6–8: 'flowerets, by the nightly chillness bended down and closed, erect themselves all open on their stems when . . .'; footnoted.

67.10 Barnes · The references below are to *Poems of Rural Life in the Dorset Dialect. Third Collection* (see 42.16 n.).

67.10–11        the wild . . . sheet · 'The Love Child', i.6 (50): 'The white deäsies, a-spread . . .',

67.12        the brook . . . slide · 'The Love Child', i.3 (50): 'the clear brook . . .'.

67.13        blocks o' rock · 'The Love Child', ii.8 (51).

67.13        a love-child · 'The Love Child', title (50).

67.14        noontide's glare · 'Hawthorn Down', i.2 (52): 'noontide's gleäre'.

67.14–15        work . . . hand · 'Hawthorn Down', ii.2 (52).

67.15–16        the vootless groves · 'Open Vields', 13 (53).

67.16–17        that her . . . place · 'What John Wer A-Tellèn His Mis'ess out in the Corn-ground', iii.7–8 (55): 'that her young feäce | Mid put a former year in pleäce'.

67.18        to sink upon · 'Sheädes', ii.3–4 (56): 'did zink | Upon'.

68.1        when the . . . vew · 'Times o' Year', i.2 (56).

68.2        a milker · 'Times o' Year', iii.5 (57): 'milkers''.

68.3        stars . . . shrinken · 'Zummer an' Winter', ii.5–6 (60): 'Stars a-
            winkèn, | Day a-shrinkèn'; cf. 42.16. In TH's note the shorthand
            = 'love'.

68.4–5      night . . . eyes · Suggested by 'To Me', ii.3–4 (61): 'Though
            evenèn darkness, an' the risèn hill, | Kept all the quiv'rèn leaves
            unshown to me'.

68.5–6      clouds . . . up · 'To Me', v.1–2 (61): 'clouds went on, | Wi'
            woone a-comèn up'.

68.7        for · 'To Me', v.2 (61): 'vor'; see next entry.

68.7–8      woone . . . a gone · 'To Me', v.2 (61): 'woone a-comèn up, vor
            woone a-gone'.

68.10 Ps. 4. et seq. · Psalms, chap. iv *et seq.* The references below are to the
Psalms, in the Book of Common Prayer (Cambridge: C. J. Clay at the
University Press, 1858). TH's copy (DCM) is inscribed in ink 'Thoˢ Hardy. |
Easter. 1861.' on the recto of the blank leaf following the front endpaper.
TH's London addresses from 1862 to 1867 are also listed in pencil on this
page.

68.10–11    set . . . trouble · iv.1; line in margin.

68.12       sorrow . . . itself · iv.3: 'the Lord hath chosen to himself the man
            that is godly'; line in margin.

68.12–14    talk . . . to —— · iv.4: 'commune with your own heart'; line in
            margin.

68.14–16    put . . . was · iv.5: 'put your trust in the Lord'.

68.16       my calling · v.2.

68.17       I . . . lips · v.4: 'the God that hast no pleasure in wickedness';
            line in margin.

68.18       lead . . . sorᵂ · v.8: 'Lead me, O Lord, in thy righteousness'; line
            in margin.

69.1        abear · This word and the two immediately below it had appar-
            ently been inscribed ahead of TH's regular progression through
            the notebook; they are separated by a line from the Book of
            Common Prayer quotations and unrelated to them. See Textual
            Notes to 69.1–3.

69.1–2      thy favourable . . . days · v.13: 'thy favourable kindness'; line in
            margin. For 'ablaze' see 69.1 n.

69.2–3      her hope . . . again · v.3: 'will look up'; for 'abler' see 69.1 n.

69.3        work love · vi.8: 'work vanity'; line in margin.

69.4        save . . . time · vii.1: 'save me from all them that persecute me';
            line in margin.

69.5        deal . . . her · vii.4: 'dealt friendly with me'; line in margin.

69.5–6      love . . . then · vi.10: 'mine enemies shall be . . . put to shame';
            line in margin.

69.6        I . . . faith · Perhaps vii.1: 'in thee have I put my trust'; line in
            margin.

69.9 Sha · Shakespeare. The references below are to *Antony and Cleopatra*, in vol. X of *Dramatic Works*; those in square brackets are to *The Riverside Shakespeare* (see 3.4 n.).

69.9        tart · 225.3 [II.v.38].

69.9        to cap · Perhaps suggested by 241.3 [II.vii.134]: 'There's my cap'. Cf. *Henry V*, III.vii.114 (*Dramatic Works*, V.387.18): 'I will cap that proverb'.

69.9        to hack · 230.11 [II.vi.38]: 'unhack'd edges'.

69.10       timelier · 231.4 [II.vi.51].

69.10–11    I . . . fortunes · 237.2 [II.vii.57]; shorthand = 'imitate'.

69.11       to lip · 224.14 [II.v.30]: 'Have lipp'd'.

69.12 Sha · Shakespeare. The references below are to *Dramatic Works*; those in square brackets are to *The Riverside Shakespeare* (see 3.4 n.).

69.12–13    What . . . on majesty · *Antony and Cleopatra*, X.247.8–9 [III.iii.17–18]; shorthand = 'imitate'.

69.14       Did . . . teeth · *Antony and Cleopatra*, X.249.10 [III.iv.10]; footnoted. Shorthand = 'imitate'.

69.15       scantly · *Antony and Cleopatra*, X.249.6 [III.iv.6].

69.15       a breather · *Antony and Cleopatra*, X.247.12 [III.iii.21].

69.15       nuncio · *Twelfth Night*, III.389.8 [I.iv.28].

70.1        To cool . . . lust · *Antony and Cleopatra*, X.181.10 [I.i.10]; shorthand = 'imitate'.

70.9 Sha · Shakespeare. The reference below is to *Twelfth Night*, in vol. III of *Dramatic Works*; that in square brackets is to *The Riverside Shakespeare* (see 3.4 n.).

70.9        For . . . idleness · 392.8 [I.v.65]; shorthand = 'imitate'.

70.10 S.R · Presumably a reference to the *Saturday Review*, which TH was reading regularly during this period (see *Letters*, I.2). The quotation itself has not been identified.

70.11 C. Reade · Charles Reade. The reference below is to volume, page, and line number of *Hard Cash: A Matter-of-Fact Romance*, 3 vols. (London: Sampson Low, 1863). The novel, under the title *Very Hard Cash*, was serialized in *All the Year Round*, Mar.–Dec. 1863, but TH, a few years later, was presumably reading it in volume form.

70.11       The wrinkled sea · I.205.26–7 [chap. 7]. Neither Reade nor TH seems to have been aware of Tennyson's use of the same phrase in 'The Eagle', first published in 1851, or indeed of Shelley's image, 'the wrinkled ocean', *Hellas*, 139.

70.12 Concoc: from Hab$^k$. · Concoctions from Habakkuk. Although TH initially wrote 'Concoc' (cf. 72.1), he subsequently erased the last three letters. The references below are to the Book of Habakkuk, in the Bible (see 23.5 n.).

70.12–13    violent . . . days · i.2: 'cry out unto thee of violence'; see also following verse.

70.13–15    she showed . . . me · ii.16: 'the cup of the Lord's right hand shall be turned unto thee' and i.3: 'Why doest thou shew me iniquity'.

70.15       her red spoilt eyes · i.3: 'spoiling and violence are before me'.

70.15–71.2  her lips . . . slacked · i.4: 'the law is slacked'.

71.2–3      the fall . . . time · Apparently TH inventions related to the preceding entry.

71.3–4      there . . . speeches · i.4: 'judgment doth never go forth'.

71.4–5      whatever . . . tell · Perhaps suggested by i.5: 'I will work a work in your days, which ye will not believe, though it be told you'.

71.5–9      the end . . . down · Apparently TH inventions.

71.10       that you . . . meek · i.5: 'Behold ye among the heathen'.

71.10–11    work sweet work · i.5: 'I will work a work'.

71.11       lips . . . place · i.6: 'to possess the dwellingplaces'.

71.11–12    you . . . haste · i.6: 'I raise up the Chaldeans, that bitter and hasty nation'; cf. 25.11.

71.12–13    ye will . . . you · i.5.

71.13–14    hasty . . . heart · i.6: 'hasty nation'.

71.14–16    marches . . . beauty · i.6: 'which shall march through the breadth of the land'.

71.16–18    the length . . . minds · See preceding entry.

71.18       how . . . possess · i.6: 'to possess the dwellingplaces'.

71.19       how . . . theirs · i.6: 'the dwellingplaces that are not theirs'. 'I. 5.' = TH's memorandum of the chapter and verse to which he proposed to return.

72.1 C. Pr̃. concoc · Common Prayer concoctions. The references below are to the Order of Morning Prayer and the Psalms, in the Book of Common Prayer (see 68.10 n.).

72.1        fair offenders · General Confession: 'miserable offenders'.

72.1        soberly · General Confession: 'sober life'.

72.2        err · Venite, exultemus Domino.

72.2        a mighty salvation · Benedictus.

72.3        forefathers · Benedictus.

72.3        day spring · Benedictus; underlined.

72.3        endue · Prayers preceding the Collects.

72.3        concord · Second Collect.

72.4        assaults · Second Collect.

72.4        adversaries · Second Collect.

72.4–5      chosen . . . lad · Prayers preceding the Collects: 'chosen people'.

72.5        governance · Third Collect.

72.5–6      a lowly . . . him · Psalm xv.4: 'is lowly in his own eyes'.

72.6–7    turned . . . gloom · Apparently Psalm xiv.11: 'Who shall give salvation unto Israel out of Sion? When the Lord turneth the captivity of his people'.

72.8    maketh much of · Psalm xv.4.

72.8    hindrance of his life · Psalm xv.5: 'it were to his own hindrance'.

72.9    money upon usury · Psalm xv.6.

72.9    shall never fall · Psalm xv.7.

72.9–10    all his . . . in · Psalm xvi.3: 'All my delight is upon'.

72.10    run . . . love · Psalm xvi.4: 'run after another god'.

72.11    inheritance · Psalm xvi.6.

72.11    lot that fell to · Psalm xvi.7: 'The lot is fallen unto'.

72.11    night season · Psalm xvi.8.

72.13–14    a feigned . . . expectance · Psalm xvii.1: 'feigned lips'.

72.14    the path of life · Psalm xvi.12. 'Ps. 15. 16.' = Psalms 15 and 16,
the two TH had worked through in detail.

72.15–17 Our separation . . . thee · The quotation is from Shakespeare,
*Antony and Cleopatra*, in *Dramatic Works* (see 3.4 n.), X.198.2–4 [*Riverside
Shakespeare*, I.iii.102–4]; line in margin (erased) by 'That thou . . . thee'. Cf.
72.17 with 10.3.

73.1–2 My becomings . . . you · The quotation is from Shakespeare, *Antony
and Cleopatra*, in *Dramatic Works* (see 3.4 n.), X.197.17–18 [*Riverside Shakespeare*,
I.iii.96–7]; cf. 75.19.

73.3 All . . . allures · The quotation is from Swinburne, 'Hesperia', in *Poems
and Ballads* (see 49.7 n.), 20 (201).

73.5–6 Those . . . grey · The quotation is from Swinburne, 'Félise', in *Poems
and Ballads* (see 49.7 n.), xxiv.4–5 (222).

73.8–9 Before . . . desire · The quotation is from Swinburne, *Atalanta in
Calydon* (see 52.19 n.), 40.14 [Bonchurch edn. 294.6].

73.10 To the . . . sun · The quotation is from Isa Craig, 'One in the
Crowd', in her *Duchess Agnes etc.* (London: Alexander Strahan, 1864), iii.6
(193): 'To deeds . . .'.

73.12 His imperfection his defence · The quotation is from Scott, *The Lord of
the Isles*, in *Poetical Works* (see 4.1 n.), V.x.18 (452).

73.14–15 You had . . . me · The quotation is from Swinburne, *Chastelard* (see
20.2 n.), 129.1–2 [Bonchurch edn. 79.2–3].

74.1–2 The pleasure . . . fast · The quotation is from Shakespeare, *Richard
II*, in *Dramatic Works* (see 3.4 n.), IV.434.3–4 [*Riverside Shakespeare*, II.i.79–80];
line in margin (erased). Cf. 31.13–15.

74.3 We three . . . thyself · The quotation is from Shakespeare, *Richard II*, in
*Dramatic Works* (see 3.4 n.), IV.441.11 [*Riverside Shakespeare*, II.i.275].

74.4 To see . . . her · The quotation is from Burns, 'Bonnie Lesley', in *Poetical Works* (see 22.10 n.), ii.1 (370).

74.5 Thought . . . truth · The quotation is from Scott, *Marmion*, in *Poetical Works* (see 4.1 n.), II.Introd.111 (102).

74.6–7 To fear . . . foe · The quotation is from Shakespeare, *Richard II*, in *Dramatic Works* (see 3.4 n.), IV.465.18–19 [*Riverside Shakespeare*, III.ii.180–1]; line in margin.

74.9 Who makes . . . shame · The quotation is from Swinburne, *Atalanta in Calydon* (see 52.19 n.), 62.5 [Bonchurch edn. 307.26]; cf. 57.13.

74.11–12 Fear . . . death · The quotation is from Shakespeare, *Richard II*, in *Dramatic Works* (see 3.4 n.), IV.465.21–2 [*Riverside Shakespeare*, III.ii.183–4].

75.1–6 Silvius . . . extermined · The quotation is from Shakespeare, *As You Like It*, in *Dramatic Works* (see 3.4 n.), III.78.1–6 [*Riverside Shakespeare*, III.v.84–9].

75.7–8 Faster . . . up · The quotation is from Shakespeare, *As You Like It*, in *Dramatic Works* (see 3.4 n.), III.79.3–4 [*Riverside Shakespeare*, III.v.116–17].

75.10–11 Who tells . . . flattered · The quotation is from Shakespeare, *Antony and Cleopatra*, in *Dramatic Works* (see 3.4 n.), X.188.19–20 [*Riverside Shakespeare*, I.ii.98–9].

75.13–15 The present . . . gone · The quotation is from Shakespeare, *Antony and Cleopatra*, in *Dramatic Works* (see 3.4 n.), X.190.14–16 [*Riverside Shakespeare*, I.ii.124–6]; footnoted.

75.17–18 The hated . . . love · The quotation is from Shakespeare, *Antony and Cleopatra*, in *Dramatic Works* (see 3.4 n.), X.195.13–14 [*Riverside Shakespeare*, I.iii.48–9]; cf. 21.8.

75.19 My becoming · The quotation is from Shakespeare, *Antony and Cleopatra*, in *Dramatic Works* (see 3.4 n.), X.197.17 [*Riverside Shakespeare*, I.iii.96]: 'my becomings'; cf. 73.1.

76.1 Hangs . . . tongue · The quotation is from Shakespeare, *As You Like It*, in *Dramatic Works* (see 3.4 n.), III.20.6 [*Riverside Shakespeare*, I.ii.257]: 'hangs these weights . . .'.

76.2 Cupid have mercy · The quotation is from Shakespeare, *As You Like It*, in *Dramatic Works* (see 3.4 n.), III.21.25–6 [*Riverside Shakespeare*, I.iii.1–2].

76.3–4 Say . . . regret · The quotation is from Swinburne, 'Rococo', in *Poems and Ballads* (see 49.7 n.), iv.5–6 (133).

76.5–7 I will . . . restorative · The quotation is from Shakespeare, *Romeo and Juliet*, in *Dramatic Works* (see 3.4 n.), VIII.244.19–21 [*Riverside Shakespeare*, V.iii.164–6].

76.9–11 Something . . . forgotten · The quotation is from *Antony and Cleopatra*, in *Dramatic Works* (see 3.4 n.), X.197.10–12 [*Riverside Shakespeare*, I.iii.89–91]; footnoted.

76.13 Some . . . man's · The quotation is from Swinburne, *Chastelard* (see 20.2 n.), 39.2 [Bonchurch edn. 27.26].

76.15 Oh, all . . . that · The quotation is from Swinburne, *Chastelard* (see 20.2 n.), 17.17–18 [Bonchurch edn. 16.16–17].

77.1 Merch$^t$ of Venice · *Merchant of Venice*. The references below are to Shakespeare, *The Merchant of Venice*, in vol. II of *Dramatic Works*; those in square brackets are to *The Riverside Shakespeare* (see 3.4 n.).

77.2–4 Ant . . . one · 444.8–10 [I.i.77–9]; line in margin.

77.6–7 Por . . . followed · 448.6–7 [I.ii.10–11].

77.9–12 Lady . . . irons · TH's summary of one of the 'Anecdotes of Dr. Johnson, by Hannah More'—derived from *Memoirs of the Life and Correspondence of Mrs. Hannah More*, ed. William Roberts, 4 vols. (London: R. B. Seeley and W. Burnside, 1834), I.200)—in *Johnsoniana: A Collection of Miscellaneous Anecdotes and Sayings of Dr. Samuel Johnson, as Revised and Enlarged by John Wright, Esq.*, 2 vols. (London: Henry G. Bohn, 1859), I.322–3. TH's copy of *Johnsoniana* is in DCM together with the eight volumes of James Boswell, *The Life of Samuel Johnson, LL.D.*, ed. John Wilson Croker (London: Henry G. Bohn, 1859).

77.16–18 There is . . . absence · The quotation is from Shakespeare, *The Merchant of Venice*, in *Dramatic Works* (see 3.4 n.), II.451.14–15 [*Riverside Shakespeare*, I.ii.109–10].

78.1 Wear . . . pocket · The quotation is from Shakespeare, *The Merchant of Venice*, in *Dramatic Works* (see 3.4 n.), II.468.8 [*Riverside Shakespeare*, II.ii.192]. For TH's note see Introduction, xiii.

78.15–16 If your . . . letter · The quotation is from Shakespeare, *The Merchant of Venice*, in *Dramatic Works* (see 3.4 n.), II.501.10-11 [*Riverside Shakespeare*, III.ii.321–2].

78.17 thy currish . . . wolf · The quotation is from Shakespeare, *The Merchant of Venice*, in *Dramatic Works* (see 3.4 n.), II.515.17–18 [*Riverside Shakespeare*, IV.i.133–4].

79.1 Much Ado &c. · *Much Ado about Nothing*. The reference below is to Shakespeare, *Much Ado about Nothing*, in vol. II of *Dramatic Works*; that in square brackets is to *The Riverside Shakespeare* (see 3.4 n.).

79.1–4 Though . . . villain · 103.11–13 [I.iii.30–2].

79.7 L. L. L. · *Love's Labour's Lost*. The references below are to Shakespeare, *Love's Labour's Lost*, in vol. II of *Dramatic Works*; those in square brackets are to *The Riverside Shakespeare* (see 3.4 n.).

79.8    She must lie here · 214.22 [I.i.148]; footnoted.

79.9    We be . . . Hand · Evidently a quotation from TH's dialect-speaking uncle Henry Hand (1807–83), his mother's eldest brother, a building tradesman living in Puddletown; there was a Chequers public house in High East Street, Dorchester.

79.10     'Tis . . . that · 231.4 [II.i.118]; footnoted. In TH's addition 'Colloq.' = 'Colloquial'.

79.11     A snip · 238.12 [III.i.22].

79.13     The four . . . play · A reference to 223.3 [I.ii.83]: 'Is that one of the four complexions?' In TH's note the shorthand = 'imitate' and 'pps' = 'perhaps'.

80.3     Edw$^{\underline{d}}$ Cox, pps · Edward Cox, perhaps. The reference is presumably to the Edward Cox, several years TH's senior, who was the youngest child of the Hardy family's Higher Bockhampton neighbour John Cox, the 'relieving officer and registrar' mentioned in the opening paragraph of *Life* (7). TH later had the registrar himself in mind as the 'original' of Tony Kytes's father in 'Tony Kytes, the Arch-Deceiver': see Simon Gatrell, *Hardy the Creator: A Textual Biography* (Oxford: Clarendon Press, 1988), 116. For a helpful account of the Cox family, see Brenda Tunks, *Whatever Happened to the Other Hardys* (Canford Heath, Dorset: Brenda Tunks, 1990), 74–7.

80.4–10     Cost. . . . great · 305.6–8, 13–15 [V.ii.550–2, 557–9].

80.12–16     Dull . . . blood · 216.4–8 [I.i.181–5].

81.2–6     Armado . . . no · 220.8–13 [I.ii.1–6].

81.8–13     Arm . . . girl · 223.28–9, 224.4–6 [I.ii.109–10, 115–17].

81.15–82.5     Nathaniel . . . it · 256.3, 6–8, 11–12 [IV.ii.62, 65–8, 70–2].

82.8–9     God . . . way · 263.3 [IV.iii.74].

82.10–18 Walpole's . . . death · TH's notes on the mistresses of George I and George II, loosely based on Walpole's 'Reminiscences of the Courts of George the First and Second' as included among the introductory materials in *The Letters of Horace Walpole, Earl of Orford*, ed. [J. Wright], 6 vols. (London: Richard Bentley, 1840), I.li–cx. See especially I.liv, lix (and n. 2), lx (and n. 1), lxi, lxiii, lxv, lxxx, lxxxvi–xciii, and xcviii (and n. 1). TH is not known to have owned this edition and 'Sept 68' is presumably the date of his reading a borrowed or library copy.

83.2–84.9 clanging . . . wave · These entries, on a leaf transferred from another notebook, are clearly TH's own experimentations, not quotations from other writers.

84.10–17 Aug. . . . thunder · Erased passage on tipped-in leaf. Since TH left London for Dorset in July 1867 (*Life*, 55, confirmed by an annotation in his prayer-book), this note, evidently made at the Higher Bockhampton cottage, could well belong to Friday, 9 Aug. 1867. Its occurrence, however, on a leaf transferred from another notebook, would seem to make Sunday, 9 Aug. 1868, an equally plausible date; by Monday, 9 Aug. 1869, TH was living in Weymouth, though doubtless making frequent visits home. The bracketed space at the beginning of line 17 (perhaps also the bracketed space at the beginning of line 13) is occupied in the original by an imperfectly legible monogram that seems related to 'Mother's House', Hardy's standard form of reference to his Higher Bockhampton birthplace: see *Biography*, 20.

85.1–2 We cannot . . . of demonstrations · The quotation is from Edward Dowden, 'Lamennais', *Fortnightly Review*, OS 11, NS 5 (Jan. 1869), p. 9, ll. 36–7.

85.3–4 There . . . Egil · The quotation is from Eiríkr Magnússon and William Morris, 'The Saga of Gunnlaug the Worm-Tongue and Rafn the Skald', *Fortnightly Review*, OS 11, NS 5 (Jan. 1869), p. 27, l. 9. Shorthand = 'might begin a tale thus'.

85.5–6 The Physiology . . . Rev$^w$ · The references below are to page and line number of H. Charlton Bastian, 'On the Physiology of Thinking', *Fortnightly Review*, OS 11, NS 5 (Jan. 1869).

85.6          the trumpet-call · 57.32–3.

85.6          acquired, then organised · 63.23: 'acquired by the child, and then organized'.

85.7–8        a system . . . thinking · 57.34–6: 'a system of articulate words . . .'. Despite TH's ellipsis and colon the passage is in fact continuous in the original.

85.9–10       parts . . . order · 60.31–2.

85.11         motor processes · 62.37.

85.11         an almost automatic act · 63.26–7: 'automatic acts'; cf. *Fortnightly Review*, 66.19: 'a veritably automatic process'.

85.12 Lamennais . . . Rev$^w$ · The references below are to page and line number of Dowden, 'Lamennais', *Fortnightly Review* (see 85.1–2 n.).

85.13         a social man · 1.23–4.

85.13–14      impassioned . . . society · 1.27–8.

85.14–16      His immense . . . natures · 2.39–40.

85.16–86.2    The passionate . . . him · 4.43–4: '. . . characterise the author'.

86.2          Unfiguratively · 5.18.

86.3–4        Lamennais . . . ideals · 5.35–7: 'Lamennais was poor, feeble in health, and burdened . . .'.

86.5–6        Indifference . . . doctrine · 7.23.

86.7          delivered with precision · 7.24.

86.8 Pym. (Goldwin Smith.) · The references below are to page and line number of Goldwin Smith, 'Pym', in *Three English Statesmen: A Course of Lectures on the Political History of England*, 'People's Edition' (London: Macmillan; Manchester: Alexander Ireland, 1867). That TH used this edition—rather than the first edition (London: Macmillan) of the same year or the 'New and Revised Edition' (London: Macmillan) of 1868—is confirmed by the recorded page references and the presence of distinctive textual variants.

86.9–11       How . . . past! · 2.13–15: '. . . and for the altars . . .'.

86.12         a compliant · 4.13: 'the compliant'.

86.12         a recusant · 4.14: 'recusants'.

86.13–15      In the . . . power · 7.33–4.

87.1–3        Mirabeau . . . Jacobins · 16.8–10.

87.4–15     I have . . . chivalry · 17.1–9.

87.16–88.8  Above . . . cause · 17.42–9: '. . . are now seen . . .'. The abbre-
            viations 'indep$^t$', 'yeom$^{y.}$', 'conq$^{d.}$', 'Eng. lib.', and 'pps' = 'inde-
            pendent', 'yeomanry', 'conquered', 'English liberty', and
            'perhaps'.

88.9–10     Public . . . so · 21.44–5: '. . . and that its titles . . .'.

88.11–14    In that . . . not · 22.32–5: 'In the vestibule of that . . .'.

88.15–16 The Saga . . . Rev$^w$ · The reference below is to page and line
number of Magnússon and Morris, 'The Saga of Gunnlaug the Worm-
Tongue and Rafn the Skald', *Fortnightly Review* (see 85.3–4 n.).

88.16–17    He was . . . been · 27.5–6: '. . . father Egil had been'; short-
            hand = 'imitate to strength'.

89.1–13 *inverted* Ask . . . Elfrid · A series of erased pencil notes, written on
the rear endpaper with the notebook turned back to front, hence upside
down: see Introduction, xiii–xiv, and Editorial Procedures, xxv.

89.1–2 *inv.*   Ask . . . what · The reference to 'Mac' is probably to the firm
                Macmillan & Co., although it could be to Alexander Macmillan
                (see *Letters*, I.7–8), or to his son Malcolm Macmillan (see *Letters*,
                I.12). For speculation as to the subject of the advertisement(s) see
                Introduction, xiv.

89.3 *inv.*     HMM · Horace [Horatio] Mosley Moule (1832–73), 4th son of
                the Revd Henry Moule, vicar of Fordington; until his death by
                suicide in 1873 he appears to have been TH's closest friend and
                literary adviser. See *Biography*, 66–71, etc.

89.5–6 *inv.*   If lit. . . . Holdern$^s.$ · Holderness, in SE Yorkshire, is famous for
                the great medieval churches of Beverley, Hedon, Patrington, etc.
                See Introduction, xiv.

89.7 *inv.*     Craik · George Lillie Craik, husband of the novelist Dinah
                Maria Mulock, became a partner in Macmillan & Co. in 1865.
                He is briefly mentioned in *Life*, 230.

89.8 *inv.*     Mark L. · Mark Lemon (1809–70), editor of *Punch* 1841–70; he
                had written for the theatre as a young man and in late 1866 or
                early 1867 (according to *Life*, 55) TH sought his advice as to the
                advisability of gaining theatrical experience as a preparation for
                the writing of plays in blank verse.

89.10 *inv.*    R. Room · Not, presumably, the Reading Room of the British
                Museum but that of a more accessible institution—such as the
                South Kensington Museum (see *Letters*, I.1) or the Marylebone
                Library and Scientific Institution (see *Biography*, 78)—where cur-
                rent newspapers and periodicals could be consulted.

89.11 *inv.*    S.R. · *Saturday Review*; see 70.10 n. Horace Moule was an occa-
                sional contributor.

89.12 *inv.*    H. of R from Mudie · The references are almost certainly to
                Charlotte M. Yonge's novel, *The Heir of Redclyffe* and to Mudie's
                Select Library. See Introduction, xiii–xiv.

89.13 *inv.*  Illustrated mythology · Probably a work on Greek mythology, but since Moule was an active reviewer the reference is conceivably to Edward Moor's *The Hindu Pantheon*, illustrated by numerous line-drawings, of which a new edition had recently appeared (Madras: J. Higginbotham; London: Trübner and Co., 1864 [British Museum accession stamp dated 8 Feb. 1866]).

89.13 *inv.*  the lady Elfrid · Elfride is the name TH gave to the heroine of *A Pair of Blue Eyes* (1873); the stress on 'lady', apparently originating with Moule, is curiously echoed in Moule's comment on *A Pair of Blue Eyes* in his letter to TH of 21 May 1873: 'You understand the *woman* infinitely better than the *lady*—' (DCM; quoted *Biography*, 150).

# Textual Notes

| | | |
|---|---|---|
| 1.1–4 | T. Hardy . . . [rule] · Ink over pencil; illegible pencil erasures at top of page, between lines 2 and 3, and below line 3. |
| 2.1–7 | Thomas . . . "——" · Pencil. |
| 3.1 | To be destroyed · Across upper left-hand corner in blue crayon (erased), the underlining in red crayon (erased). |
| 3.1 | (Pri:) · Preceded by illegible ink erasure. |
| 3.2 | Studies. Specimens &c. · Underlining over illegible ink erasure. |
| 3.3 | 1865 Notes. · Ink over erased pencil; preceded by illegible pencil erasure. |
| 3.11 | days' · Pencil apostrophe. |
| 3.11 | thee / · Virgule over full point. |
| 3.17 | me) / · Parenthesis added; virgule over full point. |
| 4.5 | Sc: · Added. |
| 4.15 | Shakes . . . thorou.ᵞ · Ink over pencil, substituting equals sign for comma after 'freshes'. |
| 5.1 | bit / · Virgule over full point. |
| 5.2 | captivated / · Virgule over full point. |
| 5.8 | thralls = · Equals sign over virgule. |
| 5.14 | ..bia / · Virgule over full point. |
| 6.1 | Wordsw. · Written above top line; perhaps added. |
| 6.4 | muffled · 'ff' over 'vl'. |
| 6.13 | laggard · 'ard' over 'ed'. |
| 6.14 | maintenance, = · Equals sign added. |
| 8.5 | coverture / · Virgule over comma. |
| 10.1 | (finished) · Opening parenthesis formed from virgule. |
| 10.4 | scope · 'c' over ascender. |
| 10.9 | roses · Followed by deleted virgule. |
| 12.15 | whom .. salutes · Initial 's' over full point; 'l' over virgule. TH first wrote: 'whom ... /'. |
| 13.8 | knot · 't' over 'w'. |
| 13.8 | untwine · 'u' over 'e'. |
| 13.12 | (good · Parenthesis over apparent colon. |
| 13.16 | (discover · Parenthesis over equals sign. |
| 13.17 | (yard) · Opening parenthesis over equals sign. |
| 14.13 | (twinkle) · Opening parenthesis over apparent uncompleted equals sign. |
| 14.17 | (bounded) · Closing parenthesis over virgule. |
| 15.1 | lay ) · Parenthesis in error for virgule. |
| 15.1 | empery ) · Parenthesis in error for virgule. |
| 15.3 | reverie / · Virgule over full point. |
| 15.5 | main / · Virgule over full point. |
| 15.7 | (within · Parenthesis over full point. |
| 15.7 | (know) · Opening parenthesis formed from virgule. |
| 15.10 | albeit / · Virgule over full point. |

15.15     stand · Pencil underlining.
15.20     [southing . . . Chaucer] · Written below bottom line; perhaps added.
16.1      Shak . . . he) · Ink over pencil.
16.5      outspring · 'o' over 's'.
16.6      scare · 'a' over 'o'.
16.8      (fine · Parenthesis over equals sign.
16.12     Skak · *sic.*
17.2      (that · Parenthesis formed from virgule.
17.6–8    Col . . . may'st) · Ink over erased pencil, substituting colons for virgules after 'fall', 'tongues', 'aslant', and 'child'.
17.14     night) · Parenthesis formed from virgule.
17.17     cannon · 'no' over 'o'.
18.13     obedient · 'be' over 'rb'.
19.4      his · 'is' over 'e'.
19.11     (overween · Parenthesis over colon.
19.14     (may · Parenthesis over colon.
20.3      all · 'al' over 'w'.
20.17     of likely · 'o' over ampersand; initial 'l' over semi-colon.
21.9      : to · Colon added, replacing original colon overwritten by 't' of inserted 'to'.
21.11     of · 'o' over closing parenthesis.
21.16     (continues · Parenthesis over colon.
21.18     (wave) · Opening parenthesis over uncompleted colon.
22.12     to · Pencil underlining.
22.16     [on] · Square brackets over parentheses.
23.2      [hence · Square bracket formed from opening parenthesis; 'hence' added over 'i.e.'
23.2      &c] · Square bracket over closing parenthesis.
23.3      [or · Square bracket formed from opening parenthesis.
23.4      [the knee] · Square brackets formed from parentheses.
24.1      Mem: · 'M' over colon.
24.9–13   Bur . . . woods · Ink over pencil, except full point after 'fr' and quotation marks enclosing 'peer it' and 'drew my gazing wonder' pencil only; in pencil version 'closed' not underlined and '∴ drew my g.' enclosed by parentheses.
25.17     height · 'e' over 'i'; 'i' added.
26.1      and · 'a' over dash.
26.2      & · Over dash.
26.12     leaf · 'l' over dash.
26.12     roll · 'r' over dash.
27.10     regret, · Initial 'r' over partly erased 'R'; comma over dash.
27.10     die! · Followed by illegible ink erasure.
27.13     feud · 'f' over 'h'.
28.13     ∴ · Added.
28.15     ∴ · Added.
28.18     from · 'f' over dash.
28.18     forgetfulness · Initial 'f' over dash.

29.13    hear —  ·  Dash over colon.
29.15    of  ·  Over dash.
29.18    (rules)  ·  Opening parenthesis over dash.
30.3    (defiance)  ·  Opening parenthesis over dash over colon.
30.6    G.T.  ·  Added.
31.7    <u>Rch</u><sup>d</sup> II  ·  Double underlining over single underlining.
31.13    (curb)  ·  Opening parenthesis over colon.
31.15    <u>fast</u>  ·  's' over 'r'.
32.6    <u>Sha</u>  ·  'h' over 'k'.
32.9    <u>himself</u>  ·  'l' over 'f'.
35.1    &  ·  Over colon.
35.2    <u>field-ward</u>  ·  Hyphen added.
35.2    : <u>to</u>  ·  Colon added, replacing original colon overwritten by 't' of inserted 'to'.
35.3    <u>gave</u>  ·  'g' over colon.
35.4    Sound  ·  'S' over 's'.
35.10    gadder ·   ·  Raised point apparently uncompleted colon.
36.4    [love  ·  Square bracket over colon.
36.7    <u>thrilling-sweet</u>]  ·  Square bracket over uncompleted colon.
36.13    her =  ·  Equals sign over colon.
38.5    ruddiest  ·  'ru' over 'w'.
38.8    unity :  ·  Colon over full point.
38.13    birds  ·  's' added.
38.16    <u>lodge</u>  ·  'd' over 'o' and uncompleted 'k'.
39.5    thy  ·  't' over colon.
39.8    my  ·  'y' over 'e'.
39.9    as at  ·  'as' added; 't' of 'at' over 's' of original 'as'.
39.10    display]  ·  Square bracket over colon.
39.11    a ....]  ·  Square bracket over semicolon.
39.14    Gaunt :  ·  Followed by illegible ink erasure.
40.11    (substitute  ·  Parenthesis over full point.
40.15    <u>Is II</u>  ·  Preceded by illegible ink erasure.
40.17    [ ⌒  ·  Square bracket formed from parenthesis.
41.2    (mien)  ·  Opening parenthesis over square bracket.
41.5    <u>captivitity</u>  ·  sic.
41.13    Sc. . . . <u>away</u>  ·  Ink over pencil.
42.1    feast :  ·  Colon over dash.
42.4–5    Sc. . . . <u>line</u> :  ·  Pencil.
42.7    after  ·  't' added.
42.12    IV  ·  Added.
43.9    (mistaken)  ·  Opening parenthesis over colon.
45.10    (heart  ·  Parenthesis over colon.
45.15    <u>Sha</u>  ·  'h' over 'k'.
46.4    <u>By:</u> to see into :  ·  Ink over erased pencil.
46.17    hour, even  ·  Comma added, replacing original colon overwritten by initial 'e' of 'even'.
47.2    the  ·  Added.
47.6    blushes  ·  'lushes' over 'Whe'.

| | |
|---|---|
| 48.1–2 | as my . . . age :  ·  Ink over pencil, except comma after 'thee' and final colon (over pencilled dash) pencil only. |
| 48.15 | (reason,)  ·  Parentheses added. |
| 48.16 | hurt  ·  Pencil. |
| 49.4 | &  ·  Over colon. |
| 49.15–16 | As . . . Lesbian  ·  Added, TH having originally begun his quotation at 'Sappho, adrift'. |
| 49.17 | swims ✷ Asterisk presumably added following insertion of 'As . . . Lesbian'. |
| 49.21 | : a privy  ·  Colon and 'a' added; 'p' over opening square bracket. |
| 50.5 | blosoms  ·  sic. |
| 50.11 | great  ·  'g' over 'l'. |
| 51.1 | me,  ·  Comma over colon. |
| 51.2 | : that has no heart :  ·  Pencil. |
| 51.10 | went :  ·  Colon over dash. |
| 51.14 | me,  ·  Comma over colon. |
| 52.1 | might  ·  'm' and 'i' conflated. |
| 52.13–14 | eyes,/ speech/ words/  ·  Virgules added; misformed 'r' of 'words' permits possible (if not plausible) reading 'wolds'. |
| 52.16 | them  ·  'th' over 'm' of original 'me'; 'm' added. |
| 52.16 | the . . .  ·  Ellipsis added. |
| 52.18 | VI  ·  'I' added. |
| 54.6 | : Meleager  ·  Colon added, replacing original colon overwritten by 'M' of added 'Meleager'. |
| 54.9 | shook  ·  's' over colon. |
| 54.14 | sud$^{y.}$  ·  Superscript 'y' and point over colon. |
| 54.14 | loosed  ·  'e' over 'i'. |
| 54.15 | watery  ·  'a' over 'r'. |
| 56.7 | eyes  ·  'ey' over 'f'. |
| 57.12 | sea  ·  'a' over 'e'. |
| 58.1–5 | amid . . . blue  ·  Ink over erased pencil, except colon after 'mind', closing parenthesis after 't. l.', and underlining of 'swings' unerased pencil only. In pencil version 't. l.' added and 't' over original closing parenthesis. |
| 58.2 | assigned  ·  'd' over 's'. |
| 58.5 | [freshly  ·  Square bracket over colon. |
| 58.6 | ( ⌐ )  ·  Parentheses pencil. |
| 58.9 | when  ·  'wh' over uncompleted 'G'. |
| 59.2 | even$^{g.}$  ·  'n' added. |
| 59.19 | enbloom.  ·  Pencil. |
| 60.1 | Sweetly . . . love  ·  Ink over erased pencil. |
| 60.4 | ⤳  ·  Over incorrect shorthand symbol for 'eyes' (as at 58.6). |
| 60.5 | §§§§§  ·  Illegible deleted shorthand. |
| 60.5 | blush  ·  'b' over an ascender, perhaps of uncompleted shorthand symbol. |
| 60.6 | Kisses  ·  Over shorthand symbol for 'kisses'. |
| 60.8 | adulteries  ·  TH's uncorrected false start, 'd' for 'a', permits the clearly unintended reading 'ddulteries'. |

60.9        regret, · Comma over colon.
60.14       striving⎫ · Word and brace pencil.
            ⎭

60.17       mouth, · Comma over colon.
61.1        braced together⎫ · Words and brace pencil.
            ⎭

61.11       cleavings · 's' added.
62.3        for · Over 'of'.
62.18       mine, · Comma over colon.
63.7        & Sw · Probably added.
63.11       themselves] · Square bracket over full point.
63.11       Sw: · Probably added.
64.1        Swin. · Written above top line; perhaps added.
65.3        comes · 'o' over 'a'; 's' added.
66.8        eye, · Comma over colon.
66.17       fulfilments, flush · Comma added, replacing original colon
            overwritten by 'f' of 'flush'.
67.11       [the · Square bracket over colon.
67.15       [love · Square bracket added; 'l' over original colon.
68.3        [my · Square bracket over colon.
68.4        day] · Square bracket over colon.
68.7        (in place of) · Parentheses added; closing parenthesis over
            comma.
68.17       (my · Parenthesis over square bracket.
68.18       her, · Comma over colon.
69.1–3      thy . . . eyes . . . looked · Beginning of each of these words
            over illegible ink erasure of TH's original brief inscription follow-
            ing each item ('abear', 'ablaze', 'abler') in his subsequently aban-
            doned alphabetical word-list.
69.5        her · 'he' over 'me'; 'r' over colon.
69.7        crumble · Pencil.
69.7        waste · Pencil.
69.7        fade · Pencil.
69.12       What · 'W' over 'T'.
70.12       Concoc · 'coc' erased ink.
70.12       Hab^k · Superscript 'k' erased ink.
71.4        speeches · Final 'e' over colon.
71.7        its · Imperfectly formed: TH first wrote 'h' (beginning of 'his'
            or 'her'?), then added 'i' and 's' without crossing the ascender.
71.12       heats · 's' added.
71.12       me — · Dash over comma.
71.12       hopes · 's' added.

71.18       ⎧own · Word and brace pencil.
            ⎩
72.2        ("said he', soberly") · Opening quotation marks added; 's.'
            expanded to 'said'; 'he' over dash; 's' of 'soberly' over closing
            parenthesis. TH first wrote: '(s. '—')'; original single quotation
            marks survive as dot of 'i' of 'said' and non-functional apostro-
            phe following 'he'.

| | |
|---|---|
| 72.12 | day time, · Comma over colon. |
| 73.5–6 | 'Those . . . grey'. · Pencil deletion lines. |
| 75.1 | Silvius . . . me. · Added above top line. |
| 75.3 | would · 'w' over 'y'. |
| 75.6 | Sha. · Here (and at 76.1 and 76.2) the 'a' is loosely formed and could plausibly be read as the 'e' of the alternative abbreviation 'She.' |
| 75.11 | speaking · 'sp' over 'ar'. |
| 76.1 | Hangs . . . tongue. · Ink over erased pencil. |
| 76.2 | Cupid have mercy · Ink over erased pencil. |
| 77.14 | & · Over 're'. |
| 77.14 | preceding · 'd' over 'e'. |
| 78.2 | ~~psalm tunes~~ · Struck through in pencil. |
| 78.13–14 | sighs . . . lip. · Pencil. |
| 79.10 | ['Tis · Square bracket formed from parenthesis; "T" over '∴'. |
| 79.13 | loveables — · Pencil dash. |
| 79.15 | (by · Parenthesis over full point. |
| 79.16 | novelist · 'i' in pencil over illegible ink erasure; 's' over 'r'. |
| 80.3 | i.e. · 'i' over 'e'. |
| 80.4 | Cost. · 't' over full point. |
| 80.11 | character · Second 'c' over 's'. |
| 82.16 | Geo II · 'II' over rule. |
| 83.1–84.17 | 77 . . . thunder · Written on recto and verso of tipped-in leaf from a different notebook. |
| 83.1 | 77 · Erased pencil. |
| 83.3 | clicking · Lower underline red crayon. |
| 83.9 | snapping · Lower underline red crayon. |
| 83.13 | slamming · Lower underline red crayon. |
| 83.16 | drumming · Lower underline red crayon. |
| 83.17 | quavering · Lower underline red crayon. |
| 83.17 | buzzing · Lower underline red crayon. |
| 83.19 | whooping · Lower underline red crayon. |
| 83.20 | screeching · Lower underline red crayon. |
| 84.2 | (waves · Parenthesis over comma. |
| 84.10–17 | Aug. . . . thunder · Erased pencil. |
| 85.1 | discover ./. · Ellipsis struck through in pencil. |
| 85.2 | Rew^w · sic. |
| 85.4 | Egil · 'il' over 'li'. |
| 85.7 | of words · Added over ellipsis. |
| 85.8 | outwardly · 'ou' added; 'w' over 'he' of original 'the'. |
| 86.13 | Right · 'R' over lower-case 'r'. |
| 86.14 | House · 'H' over lower-case 'h'. |
| 86.16 | on · 'n' over 'f'. |
| 87.1 | Mirabeau marked · In smaller writing because added to precede quotation originally begun at 'the intensity'. |
| 87.2–3 | to the . . . Jacobins · Added; TH used smaller writing, as for the previous addition (87.1), even though unconstrained in this latter instance by considerations of space. |

| | |
|---|---|
| 87.8 | lose · 'se' over 'os'. |
| 88.15 | & · Over full point. |
| 88.17 | & · Over full point. |
| 89.1 | s$^{\underline{d}}$ gladly— · Erased pencil. |
| 89.2 | 43 pp. · Unidentified hand. |
| 89.1–3 *inv.* | —Ask . . . Elfrid" · Erased pencil. |

# Index